The Secret Island

Arthur Versluis

This book is both an odyssey and an alchemical quest around the known world, a pilgimage to those numinous places marked with megaliths, dolmens, menhirs, and great stone spheres. They bear witness to another world of primordial presences that still hold an initiatic power for those attuned. Most moving is the author's return, like Odysseus, to find what he sought on his home turf.

—Joscelyn Godwin, author of *Atlantis and the Cycles of Time, Upstate Cauldron,* and many other books.

Praise for other books by Arthur Versluis

Dr. Arthur Versluis, one of the world's foremost esoteric scholars, takes us on a journey to the fabled Aegean isle of Samothrace, a center of the ancient Mysteries. This book is a travelogue, and not just in a physical sense—Dr. Versluis guides us on a journey through realms of myth and history to uncover the secrets of ancient Western spirituality. At journey's end, the author steers us home to who we really, deeply are.

—Leonard George, Capilano University, author of *Crimes of Perception* and *Alternative Realities*

Library of Congress Cataloging-in-Publication Data

Names: Versluis, Arthur, 1959- author.
Title: The secret island / Arthur Versluis.
Description: 1st edition. | Minneapolis, MN : New Cultures
Press, 2020. | Identifiers: LCCN 2020015767 (print) | LCCN
2020015768 (ebook) | ISBN 9781596500341 (trade paperback)
| ISBN 9781596500358 (epub)
Subjects: LCSH: Sacred space. | Religion and geography. |
Islands. Classification: LCC BL580 .V47 2020 (print) | LCC
BL580 (ebook) | DDC 203/.509142--dc23
LC record available at https://lccn.loc.gov/2020015767
LC ebook record available at https://lccn.loc.gov/2020015768

27 26 25 24 23 22 21 20   10 9 8 7 6 5 4 3 2 1

New Cultures Press
Minneapolis, MN
www.newcultures.org

The Secret Island

Contents

Chapter One

First Words

This book is an island. I know, dear reader, that you too are surrounded by the hubbub of the world around you and all its demands. You have to set aside time to read—not only time, but also attention. You have to tune out the noise, and hone in on the signal. And you can't do that unless you separate yourself enough to enter into this book, the world of its words and what it brings forth. It is an archaic act, this separation in order to read. Thus it's not true that no man is an island—because to read, you have to become an island. And in that way, you make entirely different connections; you live in more than one dimension; you enter into new worlds by entering that island. That, today, is a rare thing.

You might think to yourself: what sort of author is this, who addresses me as reader directly? And I admit, it is not my usual way. But we are not in ordinary circumstances, and this is not an ordinary book. It is, rather, a book in which I confide in you; I share confidences; I offer hints and indications; and it is even a kind of initiatory journey that we share together. It is a meditation in both senses of the word. It is a shared meditation. What I am sharing here isn't for everyone—it's only for you, if you choose to come along. If not, that's perfectly fine. And if you do, then it's only for you.

Allow me, at this point, to introduce a notion, not something to dwell on overmuch. I refer to primordiality. The primordial. It is an intimate dimension of this book. What does such a word mean? To what does it refer? Not time, of course, otherwise I suppose it would be construed as the very old. It isn't that. The primordial doesn't really belong to time at all, but rather is that out of which time ceaselessly emerges. Primordiality is the quality of the primordial; it is what we encounter in a primordial place.

But what is a primordial place? Of course we could say that the primordial can be experienced anywhere. However, there are some archaic places somehow both in and outside time. In Costa Rica, standing in the ocean looking back at the wild shoreline, I felt as though a dinosaur might lumber out from behind the lush jungle trees and foliage. And atop a high hill at a cairn in Ireland, from which it is said you can see a third of that green island, where the wind ceaselessly whips you, there too, I have felt primordiality. I say felt, or intuited, but how to express it? Experience. We *experience* it.

The German mystics understood what I am alluding to here. Master Eckhart and John Tauler, the greatest of the medieval mystics, both recognized that to become wise is to give oneself up to divine solitude, a secret solitude that is silence, and emptiness. This secret solitude is that of the primordial origin, the *ursprung*, they termed it. *Ur-* means "primordial;" and the word *ursprung* is akin to the ancient Platonic term *archē*. It was the greatest of the German philosophers, Friedrich von Schelling, who brought together the insights of the German mystical tradition, including those of the extraordinary mystic Jacob Böhme, and referred to the *ungrund* or not-ground that is the groundless absolute prior to all dualities, at once primordial and beyond all identification. Thus the primordial, in this tradition, could be referred to as the beginningless beginning prior to all beginning.

A few of the Romantic poets also intuited what I'm alluding to here. At least some of the Romantics, on the cusp of modernity and industrialization—the incipient technologization of the human world—recognized that in wild places we can sometimes perceive the sublime, archaic and transcendent. Their thought was that in a disenchanted society, it was necessary to go into special places in order to experience reënchantment. That is still true today—indeed, it is even more necessary today than at that time. But for us, in our technologized world, so full of distractions, it is not enough to go physically to such places. We also must divest ourselves of our diversions. We need to regard such a place as an island unto itself, a sacred place in which we do not bring all the clamor of modernity.

In some respects, Samothrace is such a place. The semi-wild goats that dot the hillsides ensure that the island is not dense with foliage, but up the mountain Saos, and above the shoreline, with the cerulean Mediterranean surrounding it, the island today can still give one that sense of primordiality. Samothraki, as it is known in Greek, is the home of an ancient Mystery cult whose origins are so far back as to be lost, perhaps belonging to the Pelasgians who were said to have preceded the Greeks themselves. The ruins of Samothrace's temple complex may still be found, and one senses, even after the lapse of millennia, that here were celebrated rites radiating primordiality still. Standing before these Samothracian ruins, the secret island first began to dawn on, or perhaps better, in me.

The Mysteries of antiquity drew thousands of initiates, yet not one divulged their initiatic secrets. Many authors have marveled at this, and it is remarkable, though one of the chief reasons may be that the secrets of the Mysteries, what was revealed in the illuminated darkness, not only should not, but indeed *cannot* be conveyed in ordinary ways. The extraordinary, the communication of and with the gods, cannot be rendered ordinary. It belongs to a different level of being. The Samothracian Mysteries were conveyed in a tongue so ancient that it was old already a thousand years before Rome became the center of the ancient world. A secret conveyed in a secret language: the abyssal word.

Standing with an ancient megalith above the windswept coast of Cornwall, there too, on that elder island I have known primordiality. It is not that such places are entirely wild, though wild they are, it is that there we experience also the timeless moment in which the stone was raised and consecrated millennia before; such a place is in some sense transparent or translucent. What was, still is, and will be. For it, in it, time both is, and is not. This is true too, in a cave marked by petroglyphs from shortly after the glaciers covered Northern Europe. Here too, in the darkness and stillness, we are in place some-how still outside time. There, the earth's heart is illuminated by the starlight of ten thousand years ago, and time has no sway over us.

I mention such places because there, among megaliths or pillars, we can experience the union of above and below, of the sky and the depths of the earth. It is not surprising that there too we may experience archaic images from the present past, and perhaps even from the present future. That is what the poet Novalis sought to capture in his magical novellas, in his magical poetry, and in his fragments. Here the primordial Word may be heard whispered in our inner ear, the primordial Image might be seen with our inner eye. Is it so surprising that in such a timeless place, a stone statue might come to life, and speak the words of the god?

Such ideas are remote from our artificial worlds of intricate contrivance. Of course, with technology one can create an artifice that speaks, but our technology's fantastic verisimilitude is at the antipode of what I am alluding to. If *their* secret island is an exquisite kind of clockwork device, *ours* is not just alive, but life itself in its purest mode. It is transparent and translucent to both time and space, not a facsimile, but a portal. For there are timeless places where we might touch eternity.

Those timeless places are what this book is about. You might consider it a kind of cartographic and cryptographic experiment. There is a key that unlocks its secrets, and when one has it, then appear the first words. The first words emerge from the abyssal depths, out of what Jacob Böhme called the *nichts*, the primordial nothing prior to all differentiation. Perhaps our words always so emerge, appearing out of the abyss whence arises and into which disappears all creative acts.

Those timeless places are the secret island, as are the works of those who have gone before us and shown us the way, Plato and Plotinus, and their fellow explorers throughout the last several millennia, right up to our own time and finally, perhaps, up to you yourself. When we read Plotinus, really read him, we are entering into a solitary communion with him, and our act of reading in communion generates our secret island, the intellectual space within which we belong, not to our own era alone, but also to timelessness, not only to our present location, but also to a new, renewed, and more profoundly understood world.

Please do join me, if you feel so called, on this journey of exploration. You don't need to leave the comfort of your own home or even that of your favorite chair. And yet for all that, we will be at risk, moving into unfamiliar and exotic terrain, daring to explore together what is outside the bounds of contemporary maps, perhaps also outside the ambit prescribed by convention, where it may in fact be a little dangerous to tread. We begin with a quest for the West, and also for those mysterious islands of the West said to exist by the ancients and in ancient folk lore from time immemorial. In short, we begin by looking for the West, and what lies to the West of the West.

Chapter Two

Mythical Islands of the West

What does it mean to say "the West"? We hear the term bandied about regularly, but almost always in a way that doesn't quite reveal what is meant. Of course, for us, the phrase has multiple levels of meaning. On one level, "the West" refers to Europe and to the European diaspora. Thus, geopolitically, the West is Europe (from Eastern to Western), but it is also the European diaspora in Canada, and the United States, including Hawaii, all the way to Australia and New Zealand. Culturally, of course, the West is always the frontier, the wild edge beyond civilization. But what we will explore here is the mythical West, the West as spiritual frontier and as the realm of mysteries, including the mysteries of death and the afterlife.

The most famous mythical island of the West is, of course Atlantis, discussed by Plato and by other classical authors, including Diodorus Siculus. Atlantis is said in Plato's *Critias* to be the land dedicated to Poseidon (each of the gods having a different land), and its inhabitants were said to be autochthonous, that is, having sprung from the earth itself. In Plato's description, Atlantis is said to be marked by circles or spheres, a wall of gold encircling the royal palace in its center, and a wall encircling the harbor; the whole is understood as in a circle as well, that is, Poseidon made "circular belts of sea and land" in which the people lived.

Although the mythos of Atlantis became the basis for various modern versions of the legend, rarely is it mentioned that in antiquity there were also other mythical islands, including Panchaea in the south, and the Heliades in the east, as well as Hyperborea in the north. Hyperborea is not always described as an island, but was so described by Diodorus Siculus in his *History*, alluding to Hecataeus (fourth century B.C.). Hyperborea was said to be beyond the land of the Celts, in the ocean, to be no smaller than Sicily, and in concert with many other sources, to be sacred to Apollo. What's more Apollo was said to come back to Hyperborea every nineteen years (a direct link to the Metonic nineteen-year lunar cycle). Atlantis was the island of the west, said to be beyond the pillars of Hercules (Gibraltar), but it was one of these four directional mythological realms.

Interestingly, Atlantis was said by Plato in *Timaeus* to be populated by a warrior culture that sought to subdue and enslave Western Europe, which was only to be saved in the end by the Hellenic people. After their defeat, there were violent earthquakes and then a flood that submerged what Plato termed Atlantis's great and wonderful kingdom. He also remarks that beyond Atlantis was a boundless continent, which could be interpreted as the Americas. Plato's description of Atlantis in *Critias* is much more detailed, and he dwells on their harmonizing with the natural world, remarking on their fecund land and bounteous produce, as well as on the magnificence of their buildings and statues, and their use of metals. They had hot and cold water, many gardens and temples, as well as areas for exercise of men and horses. They were godlike, in their early period. But as the human element came to predominate, they eventually declined into ambition, power, and violence, coming finally to be defeated and destroyed by the punishment of Zeus.

Diodorus Siculus has a different story. His version tells a myth of Ouranos (Heaven) who civilized a bestial people and taught them based on knowledge of the stars, sun, moon, and seasons. Ouranos and his consort Titaia (later named Ge, or Gaia (Earth) had many children, who were called Titans, and one of those descendants, Basileia, was known as the "Great Mother." She in turn gave birth to Helios (Sun) and Selene (Moon). Out of jealousy, her siblings killed Helios and Selene killed herself, whereupon Basileia fell into a trance and had a vision that the Titans would be punished, and Helios and Selene would ascend into the heavens. When she awoke, she told her vision in a frenzy, her hair wild, a story later retold in celebrations accompanied by kettledrums and cymbals. What are we to make of this other tale of Atlantis?

Certainly the version told by Diodorus Siculus can be understood as alluding to the ancient Mystery traditions, specifically the cult of the Great Mother. His tale recounts, in more or less human guise, the union of heaven (ouranos) with earth, the birth of the titans, and the birth of the sun and moon. Diodorus Siculus's version also emphasizes the knowledge of the stars, sun, moon, and natural cycles, which can be understood as corresponding also to the ritual calendar of the Mysteries. But the most obvious allusion is to Basileia entering a visionary state, which she recounts with wild hair, accompanied by kettledrums and cymbals in later retellings. The name "Basileia" is a feminine form of the ancient Greek word that connotes royal power and sovereignty, and is also the name of the royal palace in Atlantis mentioned by Plato in *Critias*. Virtually all of these details correspond to a notable characteristic of the Dionysian and other Mystery traditions: female initiates who, unbound from social conventions, enter into trance and visions, accompanied by musical instruments.

How are we to understand the myths of Atlantis? It is typical, in the modern era, to seek explanations in a materialistic and historical mode, but it seems clear from the myths themselves (and from the very nature of myths) that euhemerism does not shed much light on mythology. Myths, particularly those associated with the ancient Mysteries, are very clearly about about divine illumination of human beings through Mystery rites and celebrations. Through the re-enactment of the myths (rites), people engage with and themselves encounter and embody the celestial events they depict. The Mystery myths can be understood as divine revelation through cultural re-enactment, and that is precisely what we see implied in the Diodorus Siculus version of the Atlantis mythos.

Why is an island particularly appropriate here? What is it about islands, be it Atlantis, or Hyperborea, or for that matter the mysterious island of Brasil, said to be west of Ireland, that would suggest celestial or spiritual symbolism? First of all, islands have their own weather, particularly if the island has mountains. How well I remember setting out from mainland Greece toward the ancient Mystery center of Samothrace, a haze of clouds in the distance marking our destination. So too, Ireland, the emerald isle, is known for its clouds and rain. And so it would have been with Atlantis, or Hybrasil. Second, on an island one is closer to the elements, to the ever-present surrounding ocean, to the winds, to rain and storms, to clouds that hang nearly at ground level. All natural phenomena seem intensified on an island. I remember standing atop a cairn high atop an Irish mountain, from which I could see for thirty miles or more over pastoral valleys and a meandering river. All the while the wind whipped relentlessly, the banshee wind that I came to associate with proximity to spirits, the *sidh [shee]*.

But Atlantis and Hybrasil are not the only mythical islands of the West. We would be remiss were we not to reflect on the Islands of the Blessed, *makarôn nêsoi*, known also as Elysium, mentioned throughout classical sources of antiquity. Elysium or Elision was the name of the island destination of the heroes and heroines, sometimes called the "white island." Homer in the *Odyssey* mentions how Hermes guided the worthy dead past the "white rock," the "gates of the sun," and the "land of dreams" to their final island destination (24.12). Likewise Hesiod, in *Works and Days*, mentions how those humans who were closer to the gods were said to live far from the abodes of ordinary men, living "untouched by sorrow" in the Islands of the Blessed surrounded by the waters of Okeanos (Oceanus). Plato too, in *Gorgias* refers to the Islands of the Blessed where those who lived heroic and moral lives go to enjoy bliss after death. And in *Phaedo*, Plato mentions the ancient Mysteries, and how they assist in guiding the pure soul to its happy home in the Elysian Fields.

What is the connection between the ancient Mysteries and the Islands of the Blessed? Indeed, the very name *Elysium* has the same root as *Eleusis*, home of the Eleusinian Mysteries, that is, *eleu-*, as in *eleutheria*, meaning "release," or "freedom." Initiation into the ancient Mysteries was said to grant the initiate safe passage into a happy afterlife, the same as was vouchsafed to heroes and heroines, that is, those who had forged themselves during life into more-than-human people tested by life. The heroes were those who did not go to Hades or Tartaros, that is, to the land of shades, but who rather found their way to those mysterious islands where there was no suffering or sorrow, where crops grew multiple times per year, and life consisted in delight. The Mysteries brought initiates through the darkness and into the light (symbolized by the sun at midnight, says Apuleius), and thus allowed them to experience the illumination that awaited them after bodily death.

And this brings us to the symbolism of the West. Why are these paradisal islands so often associated with the West? To answer this question, we might reflect on an oral tradition in Southwestern Ireland. There, off the coast, just beyond desolate Dursey Island at the end of the Beara Peninsula—said to be home of the Cailleach—are large rocks called Bull Rock, Cow Rock, and Calf Rock. Bull Rock (sacred to Donn, lord of the dead) has an opening through which one can see the sky and water on the other side, and it is said that the souls of the dead pass through that opening on their way after death. The ancient Irish tradition was that the souls of the dead go to the West, the direction of the setting sun, a folk tradition that undoubtedly reflects something much more ancient.

As you travel down toward the lower end of the multiple peninsulas that reach out like fingers into the Atlantic Ocean, Ireland's and Europe's southwestern tip, you enter progressively more wild and desolate landscape, until finally at the tip of the Beara, Dingle, and Iveragh Peninsulas, where the wind whips the rocky landscape, you are at what is said to be the otherworldly home of the Cailleach or her and her sisters, the Cailleach being the ancient goddess creatrix of the archaic landscape of Ireland. It is said that some of the cairns at the top of Irish mountains (like Sliabh na Cailleach) were the result of the hag of the mountains dropping stones from her gathered apron. But her home was at the southwestern tip of Ireland, where the wind blasts against the rocky shore.

And at the tip of the Iveragh Peninsula, there is an island, Valentia, which like Ireland as a whole, once was blanketed in deep forests of ancient and venerable trees. In those days, long ago, Valentia was said to be home to Mogh Ruith, an ancient Druid magus who appears in ancient Irish literature as an extraordinary figure. There are all manner of stories about Mogh Ruith, some connecting him with the Gnostics and in particular with Simon Magus, who as we might recall was said to be a sorcerer himself and capable of miraculous activities. But Mogh Ruith originally was said to be a Druid magus, who had power over the elements of air, fire, water, and earth, and who was able to defeat other druids and warriors in magical battle. He was also said to have ridden (wearing a bull hide and a feathered bird-mask) a magical chariot that flashed bright during both day and night, blinding, deafening, and killing opponents. Why would such a figure as Mogh Ruith be associated with Simon Magus and the Gnostics? A feared Druid magician, he too performed miracles, the origin of which powers were obscure and numinous.

Mogh Ruith exists in the transition between different worlds, symbolized by the island he was said to call home, which belongs neither to the ocean nor to the land, but to both, fully to neither. He was said to have lived through nineteen kings, a veiled allusion to the nineteen Metonic lunar cycles so important to the ancient megaliths. Mogh Ruith was said to be blind, but blind to this world meant he could see into the next. He also lived in between the Pagan and Christian worlds, bridging those—hence the associations with Simon Magus and Gnosticism and anecdotes from the time of Christ, and his role in ancient Irish folklore of magical Munster. He moved between the ancient forests of the Druids and the more recent pastoral Ireland where the ancient traditions had receded into the background, between the regal and spiritual figures of the day, between the ancient earth mysteries and the coming of Celtic Christianity. Was he a man? Or a god? Or both? Or neither?

What is the connection between the mysterious Islands of the West, and the dead? When the sun moves to the West, the symbolism of the day's end, twilight, and the coming of the night inevitably reminds us of our life's end, its twilight, and the coming of our own night. Mog Ruith is a twilight figure, bridging the ancient Pagan ways and the Christian world that was to give way, eventually, to the cold fluorescent light of modernity. And all of Ireland, that sacred verdant isle, belongs to the twilight, for there as the poet Yeats memorably said, the veil between this world and the otherworld is more permeable there. And perhaps this is even more so of the little island off the island, down at its southwestern tip.

There is a secret island, one mostly veiled to us secular moderns. This secret island is hidden in plain sight, present but largely unseen or unnoticed, marked as it is by stone cairns and megaliths, which are not tombs, but are connected in mysterious ways to the dead. Occasionally archaeologists have discovered skeletal remains near megaliths or cairns, but more importantly, these ancient stone monuments are said in folklore to connect to the otherworld. Thus, when you hike up the long trail to the windblown cairn at the top of southern Ireland, you're at an entrance to the fairy kingdom. From the cairn, you look out over the green valley that stretches away into the hazy distance—you are on an island in the air.

The dead travel westward, over the entrained standing stones of Carnac and over the variegated standing stones of Cornwall, west with the setting sun. What does it mean that the ancestors travel west? John Pordage, the great Christian mystic of seventeenth century England, wrote at length about the different posthumous destinations that we may fashion for ourselves during life. For Pordage, those destinations are not static but dynamic, opportunities for us to continue our spiritual progress after death. We create, in this life, the conditions we experience in the otherworld, hence there is such a wide range of possibilities.

But one of those possibilities is the island paradise of the west, represented in the Buddhist tradition of Sukhavati or in Tibetan *dewachen*, the Western paradise of Amitabha Buddha. The very name "Sukhavati" means "full of bliss" (*sukha*). One has to wonder, given how far afield is found the paradisal myth of the Western island, whether beyond being a series of parallel traditions belonging both to Europe and Asia, what we are considering are actually multiple culturally inflected versions of the same reality. Perhaps there are relatively speaking many secret islands, and yet ultimately they are all more or less clear reflections of the same one.

And another way to understand John Pordage's idea of an array of posthumous destinations is that their nature and realization really reflects the subjective state of the individual. In other words, perhaps there is one posthumous reality (the island) that is *experienced* in an array of different ways, conditioned by the subjective experience of the individual. Just as in life, so in death, a dozen people might be in the same place and have twelve different experiences of it. We each experience our own island, in this world and in the otherworld. But is it possible to move between the worlds? Are there secret islands hidden close by, and we just don't see them?

Chapter Three

Secret Lands

Related to secret islands are secret lands, that is, hidden parallel worlds into which we can enter if we find the right entrance and are able or allowed to. In Tibetan tradition, it's said that there are secret lands, a popular rendition of which is, of course, in film and fiction, Shangri-La, but also more accurately, Shambhala. Shambhala, it is said, is a secret land to which only a few find entrance, and its inhabitants are much closer to immortality than we mortals in this natural world. But such legends are told in Ireland, Scotland, and Wales; they are told in Cornwall and Brittany; I have heard of similar legends from American Indian elders. Perhaps secret lands are also universal. But how do you find or enter them?

At a crossroads in wooded rural countryside in Brittany, you first glimpse them out of the corner of your eye, and then as you focus, you see that here is another, and then another. A bent dark tree trunk, cracked and wizened, with a long snout—a dragon! Then another appears—a tree limb that is a horse's head, and another—a stag. As you look more closely, you see that there are dozens and dozens of them, a naturally formed menagerie of creatures, natural and unnatural, legendary and mundane, mythical and zoological, all spontaneously formed out of the same naturally occurring tree limbs and trunks, which over time, someone or other found and brought here, to this eerie zoo. There is something a little unsettling about the place, something not quite right, as though these creatures of wood might, when the moon is right, stretch themselves and begin to move.

I mention this spectral wooden menagerie because it belongs to the same twilight world as Merlin, partly in this world, partly in another, and belonging to the realm known through tales told over the fire five thousand years ago. The menagerie, like Merlin, bespeaks a Pagan world where a dragon can manifest itself in a tree trunk or in a series of stones, undulating over and in the earth. Merlin speaks to us from the deep forest and the ancient spring, from the world of ancient gods and goddesses that can manifest themselves in the forms of ordinary mortals, giving us direction if we ask.

Merlin himself is a mysterious figure, a shapeshifter whose nature cannot be fully known. He is different in each account, but in the oldest accounts he is of two natures, his mother human, his father a non-human, making him a *cambion*. In a Christian interpretation he is said to be the son of a demon, but of course, that is very likely a way of classifying as evil what in Pagan lore may be better understood as uncanny or as numinous, that is, charged with a magical or supernatural force or power. Such power is concentrated in certain natural places—marked sometimes by standing stones, sometimes by directional orientation, sometimes by artesian springs or other flowing water, often by a high point in the area. Merlin is affiliated with such sacred places in the natural world; he is the keeper of nature's mysteries; and by his very nature, he is a bridge between those mysteries and the human world.

Merlin is a prophetic figure in some accounts; one of the earliest texts associated with him is the *Prophetiae Merlini*, or *Prophecies of Merlin*. Prophecies exist throughout the ancient world; a prophecy comes from beyond time (from the realm of the gods) into time (the human world), and concerns the interaction between these two. The word that best describes Merlin in his various guises across the many authors and tales in which he appears is *uncanny*. In one work it is said he traveled magically to Rome as a great stag in order to tell Julius Caesar that only the wild man of the woods can interpret his dream. And Merlin himself was known in some tales as the wild man of the woods, a refugee from the horrors of human society and war. What is more, Merlin is in some contexts a solitary figure; occasionally, it is said, he went into *esplumoir*, a word associated with falconry and moulting—one goes into *esplumoir* in order to return with full plumage.

But Merlin also was a lover, and in love. He fell in love with a beautiful and intelligent woman named Viviane, who asked him to teach her his magical knowledge, which he did. In some versions of the story, she tricks and imprisons Merlin, but in an important medieval version of his story, *Merlin*, the tale is a bit different. In it, Merlin's love for Viviane "grew and became stronger, so that he found it hard to leave her." And "she loved him with a deep love, because of the great nobility she found in him," so much, she tells him, that "the great love I feel for you has even made me leave my father and mother to hold you in my arms day and night." And with the magic he taught her, she fashions a "haven for joy and happiness" that endures, where "you will hold me in your arms and I you, and you will do forever what you please."

And where was this? "They tarried together for a long while, until one day they were walking hand in hand through the Forest of Brocéliande, looking for ways to find delight." The Forest of Brocéliande still exists in Brittany; there, one can still find the sacred spring where Merlin was said to have met Viviane, deep in the woods; there, one can find sacred stones and other places named for Merlin, and so it was to the Forest of Brocéliande that I went, driving there in a diesel bubble-car, down a long two-lane Breton road and into what was in fact a deep forest still, with little sign of human beings save the road itself.

As I came into this wild land of Merlin and Viviane, the hair stood up on the back of my neck, and despite the warmth of the summer day, I felt a chilly electric shock. Within a few minutes, roadside signs made it clear that I had come into the landscape of these two mysterious lovers of more than a thousand years before. I drove through the *Foret de Brocéliande* to the quaint medieval town of Paimpont, where I parked and strolled until finding a small outdoor café. I ordered an espresso, and we looked out across the square, watching people sitting together, walking, shopping. But all the while, something ancient and unfathomable was invisibly present behind what we saw.

I was living in two worlds at once. One was of course the familiar one of diesel cars and espresso machines, of cameras and people walking their dogs or sitting at a café with a friend or lover—this was the visible world of ordinary life. The other was overlaid upon or behind it, visible not only in the names, like the *Rue de l'Enchanteur Merlin*, or the *Rue de Roi Arthur*, nor only in the ancient stones of the buildings and the placid lake waters of the *Étang de Paimpont* near where we sat, nor even only in the standing stones and sacred artesian springs or huge trees hidden in the surrounding forest, but behind all these, in the accumulated lore of more than millennia, from before modernity, before Christianity, before the Romans, the secret knowledge of the Celts and the Northern Tribes, the invisible knowledge held in the landscape itself from before recorded history began.

Here, Merlin and Viviane were not only legendary, but also present, those courtly lovers, an ancient magus and his beautiful enchantress. Often on this journey, I experienced this enchanted dimension of "ordinary" life, this sense that what we were seeing might appear to be ordinary, but in fact also possessed an extraordinary dimension. I had experienced this before among Native American friends, especially when I was traveling to Native American sacred sites. A hawk perched above us, or another animal, was perhaps an animal, true—but also was a revenant from an invisible world of dreaming, where symbol and the visible converged. This hieratic dimension was especially present when going to some of the most charged sacred places, and it was so present also because the outward journey was also an inward journey.

All of this is woven into the courtly love tradition to which belong some of the stories of the love of Merlin and Viviane. In courtly love, which is a Platonic tradition, the lover recognizes the beloved as divine, or as divinity. This tradition goes back to Plato's dialogues of course, to *Phaedrus* and to Plato's idea of ascending through love, in which the lover is an initiate and initiator, in which our lover opens up a magical world where we begin to see the divine through this world. It is in courtly love as though this world becomes transparent and our beloved becomes a kind of divine sun or illumination for us.

Romance between an individual man and woman irrespective of their families is a long-standing trope in the West, often tragic, as in the cases of Tristan and Isolde, Abelard and Heloise, Romeo and Juliet—but not always so. Still, perhaps there is an element of tragedy in all romances. After all, enduring love is at odds with the fleeting nature of human life. In Asia, the arranged marriage has been common for centuries, sometimes for political reasons, sometimes for economic, often for astrological ones, too, and in such cases, the decision comes more from the families than from the individuals. The romance, and especially the courtly love tradition in which the beloved is also the divine, is distinctively Western.

The loving tenderness of lovers is evoked by a simple touch, by a glance, by a sense that this unique other person, my beloved, is a portal into unfathomable space, into mysteries that only lovers share. This love is so strong that its bliss aches in the heart. Part of this ache is from our human fragility, for in such a love we are ascending, "growing wings," as Plato put it. And it is virtually impossible to be apart, not only in the ordinary sense that we want always to be together, and that we want to join physically but also in an openness, a circulation through and between us.

Modern lovers, like Merlin and Viviane long before, walked "hand in hand through the Forest of Brocéliande," looking for the Fountain of Barenton where those two lovers had met more than a thousand years before. Walking down a wide walkway beneath the arched limbs of shade trees, and then along a winding stream, we followed it up a gentle slope through the deep woods of Brocéliande. There were no signs; there was no indication if we were walking in the right or the wrong direction, and I grew doubtful. But we continued on up the winding trail, until we crossed over and there, just ahead in a clearing, was the fountain itself, surrounded by a stone escarpment.

The fountain was surrounded by women, mostly middle-aged and elderly—occasionally there was a girl and a boy with their father and mother, or a young couple who came to pay their respects too. And pay their respects they all did: I was surprised to see that nearly everyone dipped a hand in the cool, pellucid water of the artesian spring and put water on the crown of their head. We took photographs of the water, of Merlin's rock, of the headwaters, but I also observed the people, and recognized that the women there had a protective dimension; sitting there around the edges of the spring, it was as if they were keeping watch over it, and the people, mostly French, were not tourists but Pagan pilgrims.

And what we were all in touch with, in our different ways? The fountain was long held to have magical power of healing, of changing the weather, of breaking drought and bringing rain, so by dipping their hands in the flowing stream, these pilgrims were in touch with the sourcewaters of ancient legend. The story of Merlin and Viviane was imprinted into the landscape here, and that landscape had its own profound and mysterious qualities—one cannot separate the ancient stories from the mystery of the place itself. As we stood back from the fountain among the nearby trees, I could see a ceaseless invisible flow above the fountain, a kind of irradiating power, and I knew that this was why the fountain was still revered after all these countless generations. One approaches with a natural reverence. And by going to such a charged place, we were in touch with not only what we saw, but with an origin-point of the archaic West itself.

A thousand years ago, a man named Wace, who had heard the legends, came to Brocéliande to investigate. He came expecting to find faeries visible, myths come alive, and he was chagrined to discover that there was nothing especially noteworthy about the place—or at least, he said, he came there a fool and he left there as one too. But what does it really mean that one who came seeking magic did not find it? The Druids and other magi, and indeed, the inhabitants of Gaul, Britain, and Brittany, were widely reputed by the Roman historians to have been learned in magical lore and practice. It became almost a commonplace that there was a link between them and the Pythagoreans, not least because they shared a belief in reincarnation and knowledge of sacred numbers and astrology. But perhaps there was nothing for one who was not prepared or able to see past what can be grasped with the hands, as Plato once put it.

According to the Vulgate *Merlin*, the couple Merlin and Viviane created a haven of joy and happiness that is not limited by time, and in some versions of the Merlin tales, she or he creates a magical (or physical, but also magical) house that then is his abode under the waters of a lake, whereby Viviane is sometimes known in the Grail saga as the Lady of the Lake. It is when we think about the symbolism of these story-myths that we begin to see their significances: the lovers, Merlin and Viviane, also magi, create with their love a place or haven outside time, and hidden in nature, wherein they can hold one another and be together.

And there is something about Brocéliande I need to mention here. Not far from Paimpont is *Le Val sans Retour*, the vale of no return, sometimes held to be an enchanted land in which Morgan le Fay held her lovers. Morgan was Arthur's sister or half-sister, and her name, "le Fay," means "of the faeries." Hence it is little surprise that Morgan has some of the same doubleness as Merlin—like him, and for that matter like Viviane, she is sometimes "good," and sometimes "evil;" like these other sorcerers, she doesn't fit a Judeo-Christian moral binary. According to Gerald of Wales, Morganis magically transports Arthur to Avalon, and is undoubtedly a revenant of an ancient goddess. In Geoffrey of Monmouth's *Vita Merlini*, when Arthur is wounded, he is brought to the mysterious Isle of Avalon, where Morgan is the chief of nine magical sisters, and helps Arthur heal.

I walked past the lake of the fairies, and down a trail through the woods, then up along a high ridge, past large stones that looked out over the forested hills and the lake below. One stone outcropping is called "Merlin's Seat," and indeed, it looks like a seat for a giant to look out over the valley; another is said to be the rock where Morgan was said to have entrapped her lovers, and where they would remain with no sense of time, held there by an invisible wall. These are natural stone formations rather than *menhirs*, but there are menhirs in the area as well; on a ridge nearby are the standing stones of Viviane, and not too far away is what remains of the standing stones now called "Merlin's Tomb." This whole area is numinous, and I realized, walking past Merlin's Seat, from which the sorcerer could watch the sun set, and Viviane's Rock, that the valley and indeed, the region, exists in multiple worlds at once: in it, the ancient Celtic-Druidic past, the Arthurian legends, and sacred landscape recognized in far antiquity, all converge. The very landscape here is numinous.

As I walked back toward the lake called the Mirror of the Fairies, I recalled the Tibetan legendary hidden kingdoms. In the Himalayas, it is said that there are valleys in and to which there is a hidden entrance, and once in, one finds a timeless and utopian land ruled by a benevolent king and queen. There are prophecies about such hidden kingdoms as refuges when the outer world is embroiled in the chaos, war, and confusion of the iron age, the last cycle before the renewal and a new golden age, when things fall apart and anarchy is loosed upon the world. In such a time, these hidden kingdoms are a refuge for those destined for them; here, the cultural and natural destruction never happened. Such hidden lands are at least partly outside of time; they are secret earthly paradises accessible only to those who are destined for and worthy of them.

Isn't Brocéliande itself such a place? After all, it hasn't changed much from thousands of years ago. Or perhaps a place like *Le Val sans Retour* is an entry point into such hidden lands. Perhaps that's one of the secrets of these recurrent links throughout all these characters and stories in the Grail legends, between lovers, magic, the realm of the fairies, and hidden lands or dwellings that others cannot see. When Merlin willingly enters the magical realm created by Viviane, or the "glass castle" sometimes said to be under a lake, perhaps it is a coded way of alluding to a magical realm in nature that's outside of our ordinary sense of time, a kind of portal into eternity.

But you know, there's a common theme that's often overlooked also linking all these stories. Love. Even Morgan le Fay, but certainly Merlin and Viviane. Deep love creates a magical realm partly outside of time—isn't that what the stories are really about, at least in part? Of course, there is also a legend that *Le Val sans Retour* as it now is known is not the real valley of no return—that in fact there is another valley that is the "true one." And perhaps this is a sly way of letting us know that this recurrent theme of hidden castles, hidden kingdoms, hidden realms, sometimes of the fay, sometimes of magical construction, is present in this landscape. But there is something more.

For when we look at this sacred place from above, as from the stars toward Earth, we see something remarkable. *Le Val sans Retour* can be envisaged as a point on the head of a dragon, and in fact, the sacred points of Brocéliande, including the sacred artesian springs of Barenton, and of the Fountain of Youth, when joined by a line, form a shape corresponding to the constellation Draco. And in Draco was the pole star at the time most of the megaliths were raised; in some versions, Draco was much larger than today, encompassing both of the Bears [Ursa Major and Ursa Minor], hence known as *Arctoe et Draco.* Might the name "Arthur" be related to the North [Arktos] and to the Bears, as well as to the Dragon?

And so we are reminded again of the dragon of the megaliths of Carnac, undulating across the landscape, and now find again, unexpectedly, here in Brocéliande. What are we to make of the fact that King Arthur's father's name was Uther Pendragon? The word "pendragon" is said to mean "dragon's head," or "chief of the dragons," (*caput draconis*) a name also, incidentally, for the north node of the moon (where the ascending moon crosses the ecliptic), which in turn is linked to eclipses. The south node of the moon is *cauda draconis*, or "tail of the dragon." A solar eclipse occurs when the moon's passage through a node corresponds with the new moon; a lunar eclipse occurs when passage coincides with the full moon. The lunar nodes are on a precessional cycle that lasts 18.59, or close to nineteen years, also called the "draconitic cycle."

I felt a chill when I began to realize what we were encountering. It had begun to dawn on us that in our journey, we were joining with a whole interconnected series of mysteries from great antiquity. It's like making contact with electricity: it is as if it doesn't exist at all right up until contact is made, and suddenly, the electricity flows. We plug in. That's exactly what it felt like: in Brocéliande, as soon as I entered its *nemeton*, or sacred precinct, that I was in touch with realities beyond what one can grasp with the hands. What I did not realize yet was just how much this was the case, or how deep and high were the mysteries.

This was a quest. It began by seeking to encounter directly and understand the enigmas of the megaliths, but soon I realized that the mysteries of the West were intimately tied not only to the megaliths that stand in such extraordinary profusion on the Western coast of France, but also to the myths of the Grail cycle. Yet what linked all of these? I had begun to see that the Grail cycle and in particular Merlin and Viviane, whom I felt to be in some sense real, represented a new constellation of much more ancient Celtic and Northern tribal knowledge and traditions. The Grail cycle brought the ancient Pagan traditions of the West into medieval Europe in a new way. But what were its meanings? I felt deeply connected to it, and to these mysterious figures from the distant past, but didn't fully see why.

There is another kind of secret kingdom, perhaps related, that of the faery. When you visit a cairn, piled high with stones, embedded in it a passageway with three chambers inside, what are you visiting? Is it, as folklore has it, an entryway into the realm of faery? What are the faery, anyway? It is said that the faery have their own realm, invisible to humans for the most part, in which time is elongated in comparison to ours. They have their own dwellings, roads, domestic animals, an entire faery world hidden from ours but said to be just as real. How is it that their realm can be entered through this ancient cairn atop a mountain, from which the entire surrounding region can be seen?

I was acting on intuition. But intuition was backed by knowledge. I began to realize that the West coast of France was as much a source and setting for the Grail traditions as was England, and that there were very strange links between the two West coasts, that of France and of England. From our garrulous grandmother landlady—who had learned Breton over the past decade, and who proudly told us many local legends about the standing stones and various sacred places in the region—we learned that the Breton language was actually linguistically linked to Cornish, the language of Cornwall, the Western coast of Britain. And of course even the names were linked: Barenton, Bel-Nemeton, Breton, Bretagne, Brittany, Britain. Both coastal lands were the site of Grail legends; both long have had reputations for "superstitious" folk; both have retained their distinctive rural and ancient character and traditions. But what was the meaning of all the connections between them? We won't leave Merlin, Viviane, and the Grail myths behind, but rather will take them along across the waters of the Atlantic to another ancient coast, that of Western England.

Chapter Four

The Desolated Kingdom

They call them the Rollright Stones, but also refer to them as the King and his Councilors, because across the road is a tall standing stone, the King Stone. And on the southern side of the road, behind a line of brush, stand the circle known as the King's Men. The stones are a kind of eroded limestone, not the more familiar quartz-flecked granite, and these stones are "corroded like worm eaten wood" "by the harsh laws of Time," as William Stukeley put it. They are less enduring and a bit more sinister than the granite stones; they "strike an odd terror on the spectators." These were the first standing stones we'd visited in England, and they introduced us to an ancient pattern that we find also in the Arthurian Grail tradition, writ in the heavens, of the king and the queen, and of the king and his councilors.

I stood there with Paul and Charla Devereux, who told us of the stones' history, of how there originally were far fewer stones in the circle, but some were added in the late nineteenth century. Paul has published many books on the standing stones and earth mysteries of England, and the two of them have also conducted workshops and other events; they have decades of experience with standing stones across England. As I stood near the Rollrights, the Devereuxs told of local Pagan ceremonies among the stones, some innocuous, others perhaps less so. As we walked the circle and stood at its edge, we looked out over the long high country. The lay of the land reminded me of Native American sacred sites I had visited, also on high country with great vistas and, down below, a river.

Paul and Charla, partly in reaction to New Age interpreters of the standing stones, had over the years become inclined toward more archaeological and scientific approaches to British sacred sites. Yet they also had practiced incubation—sleeping near the stones and seeing what came to them in dreams—something that had been common in Greek and Roman and Pagan Northern antiquity. There are many stories of sacred serpents or dragons or gods coming to seekers in dreams, sometimes forewarning them of some danger, sometimes wrapping around and healing them, sometimes revealing a hidden truth. I wondered what would happen were one to practice this. Paul had become a bit of a skeptic over the years, and he and Charla told us that, with regard to the mysteries of the standing stones, there was no grand solution to the enigmas they posed. Each set of stones was its own enigma with its own distinct and individual characteristics.

But it was the theme of the king and his councilors—or the king and the knights of the round table—that became the leitmotif of our journeys in England. I had encountered this theme first in Brittany, where there was often a single stone and then nearby a dolmen or a circle of standing stones, and a similar pattern was visible also here, at the starting point of the Rollrights. And it was to be seen also throughout the standing stones of Cornwall. The Cornish coast, the Western coast of England looking out over the Atlantic toward the New World, was the twin of Western France. Both were the Western Coast of Europe; both were the home of Arthurian legend; both respectively were home to the twin languages of Breton and Cornish; and both lands were renowned for their legends and mysteries, their occult inheritances from Pagan antiquity. These lands, the Western lands of Cornwall and those of Brittany, were redoubts of Celtic tradition long after Christianity had been overlaid upon neighboring lands.

I stayed in a Cornish home high above the coastline of St. Ives, an old port town that looked directly out on the Atlantic. St. Ives was renowned for the quality of its light—it was home to painters for the past century or more for just that reason—it is picturesque for that reason alone. The ocean along the harbor and shore, seen from above, was a bright, translucent turquoise much more common to Caribbean islands than to the far coast of England. Nowhere else does one find that peculiar quality, and on that first night in St. Ives, I walked down to the shore, descending on a narrow, circuitous dirt path to the ocean, under the white luminous light of a rising moon behind, the waves of the ocean ceaselessly crashing whitely ahead in the evening coolness after a red and golden sunset.

I spent the night on a high bed that overlooked the shoreline and bay, the ocean's silvery edge far below to the north. And in the morning, after a leisurely breakfast of yogurt and grapefruit, whipped eggs, and hot coffee, I drove down the coast along winding roads through Zennor, a picturesque Cornish town nestled down in a vale, and on to the standing stones of the Cornish moors. I'd become accustomed to hiking for miles through thorny bracken to find standing stones, to driving down narrow roads with poor maps, looking for indications or for telltale glimpses of vertical grey-brown rock, and these things were even more characteristic of our travels through Cornwall.

I hiked to the *Men-an-Tol*, a well-known round stone circle near which was a vertical standing stone, and although photos make them seem large, in fact it seemed to us they belonged more to faeries than to humans. I wondered if the round stone corresponded to a *yoni*, and the vertical stone to a *lingam*, for they did look like they might well symbolize female and male. In local legend, it's said that climbing through the hole in the round stone might heal one, or for women, encourage fertility, but as I stood there, and then walked on further to a nearby abandoned mine, I wondered anew about the purpose of these standing stones here in the wasteland. They did not fit standard notions of sacred sites.

In fact, the Cornish landscape as a whole did not correspond to Brittany, which seemed a green utopia, housing hidden valleys and forests and springs that had not significantly changed for thousands of years. Here, the landscape seemed desolate, the vista striking where one could look out over the ocean from above, but inland, especially on the moors, wild and forsaken, remote and forbidding. Perhaps this was the source of the legends of Cornwall, the tales of witches and faeries that often had a sinister dimension. St. Ives was luminous, but wherever else I went, the standing stones and the towns and dwellings were under grey skies and mist.

I traveled out to the very northwestern tip of the Cornish peninsula, to Pendeen and its lighthouse marking the point where ships would turn south to round the edge of Cornwall. I went hunting there for a *Fogou*, an artificial cave dug into a hill high above the ocean, and hiked through cattle pastures and along the high hills above the shore. Everywhere were stone walls made of rocks heaped up by hand over centuries, and the *Fogou* was only a different form of this. I had wondered whether it might have been an initiatic cave through which one crawled into the earth, or from the earth's heart out into the light, but once there, I began to think that the archaeologists were right—that it was but a kind of fruit and storage cellar for winter a thousand years ago.

Why had I come to Cornwall after all? I began to wonder. But I so enjoyed the search for the next set of standing stones, the next sacred site, the next spring or high vista, that such questions remained submerged beneath the ceaseless questing. Just as in France, so in Cornwall, I had learned to bring along culinary adventures, cheese and wine, nuts and fresh fruit, so even though there was rarely a suitable restaurant, I still ate well on the boot of our rented Skoda. The Skoda was not the most reliable of cars; sometimes its windows would not go up or down, and sometimes its doors would not lock or unlock. But it never left me stranded, even in the most remote two-track in far-off sheep country, and it provided a good enough picnic table on the way.

I drove to the harbor town of Penzance, with its dark stone harbor walls and ramparts, not that much changed from when the Barbary corsairs came through and sacked it in the seventeenth century. This is a part of Western history now largely forgotten—but there was a time when the Barbary pirates, sailing corsairs from the African coast, were the terror of the Atlantic, sacking towns, stealing, and taking slaves from Ireland and Iceland and England, hauling their captives back to North Africa to be sold into white slavery. It is a strange and wild chapter of Western history, and thinking of it reminds us, especially in the desolate and windblown highlands of Cornwall, of the fragility of what we often take for granted as ordinary life. What must it have been like to be set upon by such men! Little wonder that the first American war overseas was undertaken on the orders of Thomas Jefferson against the Barbary pirates at the turn of the nineteenth century. As we looked out on the town of Penzance and its harbor, we thought about another West, that across the Atlantic.

But we were here in Cornwall, and determined to begin to understand its enigmas. There were many standing stones in Cornwall, but they had an entirely different ambience than those of Brittany. What was their purpose? They did not seem to be standing guardian as those of Brittany were. And there was something else. Some of the sites seemed bereft, as if a living link had been cut, and all of the sites had a desolated quality—as if, on the peninsula called "Land's End," reaching out like a hand into the Atlantic, it was all in some sense waste land, or laid waste. The poetry of Eliot came to mind, the recognition that here, ancient and Pagan Britain was still present, but the dry stones gave no sound of water, and we were left not with living myths but with a heap of images.

There was something strange about this pilgrimage in Britain that distinguished it from France. In France, there were other pilgrims, even avatars who, in human form, guided us in the right direction. An elderly Breton in his garden, pointing us back to a dolmen we had driven past, wizened crones in jogging shoes and clothes, pointing us toward the Pagan spring—but in Cornwall, it was different. Often we had a hard time finding a particular set of standing stones or a quoit (a dolmen)—no map is sufficient, I've found. Always one has to navigate by intuition. And I soon learned, too, in Cornwall, that asking passersby did not mean that we would receive assistance. Sometimes, quite the opposite.

I was seeking a dolmen called Trevethy Quoit, the last set of stones we were looking for on a grey, misty day, under a gentle rain. But where was it? We drove to where a two-track went into the backcountry, and even followed the trail a bit in our beleaguered Skoda, occasionally scraping its bottom on hard ground and rocks, but could not find it. And as we came into a little village near it, the postman came by near us, so I asked him about it. "Never heard of it," he said. "I can't help you." Within half an hour, I'd found it, and stood beneath its impossible angle and massive weight—it was marked with a parking spot and a plaque, right near a row of houses and yes, right on the track a mailman would have to take, visible from the road. Is it possible that a mailman would fail to know a large dolmen on his own mail route? And if he did know where it was, why would he lie? What would be his motivation?

But the dolmen itself was also a mystery. It stood there, like a ramshackle shed made of huge stone slabs held together at impossible angles, one wall having fallen down a thousand years before, the others holding their own, though how, one could not guess. How did a large square slab stay at a slant above the other stones for so many millennia? It had defied gravity for five thousand years. Was it built for the spirits of the dead? And this testament to Pagan antiquity stood, as it had for millennia, now right next to a row of proper English houses and a road, as if an ancient warrior clad in fur and metal were to be standing at a railway station or in an airport. It was not like a similar dolmen in France, where part of the stone entryway had been seamlessly incorporated into a farm building adjoining it. Here, there was a discontinuity, an incongruity.

And that was what the postman was conveying to us. He was not the only one who did so. Whereas in Brittany, our landlady regaled us with stories of Pagan Bretagne, in Cornwall, we found people often sought to dissuade us from finding standing stones. Driving through a town near Bodwin Moor, we stopped to ask a heavyset local woman who was out walking in the afternoon sunshine where a well-known set of standing stones was, because the map we had indicated it, but not with sufficient precision. "Why would you want to go there? It's not worth the trouble," she told us. "It's just a few stones standing there, nothing to look at, and it's quite hard to get to. People are always disappointed."

There was some truth in what she said, of course. But we would not be dissuaded, and drove our little East European car down a long narrow road alongside stone walls, past cattle pastures, into wild high country populated by occasional groups of cattle, sheep, or goats. The countryside here in the high moorland resembled that of the American West, perhaps Montana or Wyoming, desolate country in which the cattle gave every indication of not having seen strangers recently. They eyed us suspiciously, and kept their distance as we parked the car and began to walk alongside a fencerow for what became first one mile, then two. In the distance, I could see a farmstead, isolated and still, nestled in a valley. We stayed near the fencerow so that if the bull charged us, we'd have a way out; and as we walked, the clouds began to drizzle.

As the drizzle continued, I found my way first to a single standing stone, then to a narrow apparently ancient trench that ran on a southwest to northeast angle toward an island of what looked like an old, abandoned excavation site in the middle of the cow pasture. That unimpressive site was marked by the olive-colored leaves of some low bushes, indicating that the cattle didn't go there, and as we approached, we could see the standing stones in an open indentation in the earth, some lying down, others still standing. The wind blew and whistled around our heads, blowing off my wide-brimmed oilskin hat. We had arrived—it was the place marked on the map as "King Arthur's Hall."

I had learned to check the orientation of a site with a compass, and we could see how it was aligned with peaks both to the south and to the north. What's more, I could see an orientation that had become familiar—a single standing stone off to one side, then the central site, in this case, two rows of jagged stones and an open grassy plateau between them. It was a high, windblown, desolate site, though, and its purpose, even its provenance wasn't at all clear. Were it not for the single stone and the ancient trenched earth off to the side, I'd half suspected that the whole was created with a bulldozer and a backhoe thirty years before. Could we imagine this as a knight's hall? Perhaps, but only with effort. Were such sites named recently, and only out of deference to the Arthurian legends? We wondered.

There were standing stones, dolmens, and other stone configurations scattered throughout Cornwall, and as, from day to day, we traveled to more of them, it became clearer still that even though they still stood, just as did those in Brittany, and were a familiar part of the local background, something was different about them. They seemed discontinuous, discrete, each belonging to its own isolated locale. I took striking photos of the Blind Fiddler and other, similar phallic stones standing alone in the high fields, lonely sentinels from another age, and there was sometimes a melancholy look to them, other times a sense of stoic remove. I began to think that they, and the countryside itself, had been abandoned in some profound and unseen way.

It went beyond abandonment. During the period of religious turmoil in England in the late medieval and early modern periods, the ancient Pagan traditions largely were banned, and local priests and, later, ministers took it upon themselves to go out or to encourage their parishioners to go out and destroy or deface standing stones. Beyond those renegades who pulled down and in some cases broke apart great stones, much destruction took place almost incidentally, as those building houses, churches, walls, barns, or sheds disassembled, sometimes broke, and incorporated standing stones or other ancient configurations.

A deplorable example is the great earthwork and megalithic constellation at Avebury, or Abury, as it was sometimes known. Aubrey Burl tells the story in "The Destruction of Avebury," describing how, in the early fourteenth century, probably urged by a local priest, parishioners went out and pulled down quite a few of the huge standing stones, an unfortunate barber being crushed beneath one of them. Probably it was during this time that some of the stones acquired names like "the Devil's Chair," or "the Devil's Quoit [Coyte]." Within a short time thereafter, many in the village died of the plague—and regardless of whether one sees a causal connection, those of the time might well have. It was not uncommon that standing stones were protected by local legends, by the belief that if one damaged the stones, one's crops might fail, one's animals might die, one might fail to prosper, get some disease, or even die. Such anathemas no doubt protected many of the standing stones that still dot Britain, and are to be found across Cornwall as well.

But the destruction of Avebury was not limited to the fourteenth century. The worst desecration took place with the advent of Protestantism in England, especially in the turbulent seventeenth century. Aubrey Burl writes that in the 1670s and onward, "the destruction of stones was proceeding with almost maniacal zest." A host of local "stone breakers" or "stone killers" descended upon the great sarsens of Avebury, farmers, fanatical parishioners, and would-be real estate developers, who would topple the stones, heat them with flaming straw, and pour lines of cold water upon them, then striking them with sledgehammers. In this way, innumerable standing stones were ruined. A well-known stone killer, Thomas Robinson, destroyed many stones this way to build houses, but with the poetic justice of fate, he was bankrupted, in part by the unexpectedly high cost of the demolition work.

And the destruction continued into the eighteenth and nineteenth centuries. Aubrey Burl tells of how a team of men set about destroying standing stones on behalf of the Road Commissioners, and a gentleman who observed the group at work told the foreman that men who do such things "do not deserve to die in bed." And indeed, shortly thereafter, we are told, the foreman hung himself. Such apocryphal and sepulchral tales indicate at the least some continuing adherence to the age-old sense that the standing stones are disturbed at one's peril. And they illustrate the gulf between contemporary and archaic Britain. It is true the stones still often stand, but there is a discontinuity between when they were raised and now. That discontinuity we can describe in a word as "modernity."

How is it that archaic Britons lived much as Native Americans did, raising stones and building earthworks much as they did—recognizing, in other words, sacred earth and the sacredness of some places—and yet today, the very idea seems incongruous to most? What accounts for the abyss between their world and ours? When we look at the archaeological record, we see how far afield one finds menhirs, dolmens, and other configurations of stone, across Europe, across all of Great Britain, over a span of more than several thousand years. It appears that there was a widespread knowledge of standing stones, of why and how to make them, of how to orient them toward the sun, moon, and constellations. But the knowledge seems to have disappeared completely.

And yet it is more than disappearance. Not too many years ago, someone covered the Men-an-tol stones with pitch and set them ablaze, and one can still see the smoke upon them.

Those stones still stand, but thousands upon thousands of other standing stones were destroyed over the past several centuries, throughout the modern era. In more than a few cases, it was a utilitarian farmer who didn't want the stones blocking the tilling of the soil, or cluttering up a pasture—or alternatively, wanted like Thomas Robinson to use the stones in some building or another. But one cannot ignore entirely the role of Christianity in the destruction of megalithic Britain.

The truth is that monotheism represented from the beginning, and still represents, an uncompromising rejection of Pagan (literally, "country") inheritances wherever they may be found. In the Old Testament, the Israelites are commanded to "utterly destroy" other peoples, to "show no mercy to them," to "break down their altars and dash in pieces their pillars," to "hew down their sacred trees." So were the Jews commanded, and a similar absolute rejection of Pagan traditions is visible in some forms of fundamentalist Protestantism, as also in fundamentalist Islam. It is interesting that monotheism in its various forms so often serves to divide peoples from their own inheritances, to obliterate their past, to "dash in pieces their pillars." One thinks here of the Taliban, dynamiting the great Buddha statues of Bamiyan, annihilating a world treasure, and why? For what? It is a kind of madness, one more extreme, but not dissimilar to the overturning and breaking up of the stones in Britain.

Something more ancient than Christianity calls to us. But can we hear it? I had encountered it in Brittany. And here in Britain I was confronting the Western separation from it. Something had happened in the West, something had happened to the West, to Westerners, and it was closely tied to the emergence of Protestantism, a late form of monotheism that reverted to the Old Testament template of division from and indeed, of destroying the Pagan past.

I had grown up with this sense of separation from sacred nature. In a farming family, notions of sacred nature or timelessness recognized in nature were remote from us. For us, as my cousins used to say with joking, ironically self-aware fervor, "time is money." Of course we were fortunate—we were surrounded by and lived close to the land. For most people, wild nature was remote, part of a visit to the seashore as a child, perhaps, but not part of daily life. In our farm family, we grew up without even the concept of sacred land or sacred landscapes, let alone standing stones. What did they mean? What was their purpose?

On a cloudy, grey, drizzly day in Cornwall, I stood among the standing stones of Boscawen-un, a well-known, deserted circle in the remote countryside. I parked the car and hiked back, through a gate and down a trail that meandered through thorny brush and wildflowers, past the tumuli called "Creeg Tol," to where the nineteen stones of Boscawen-un stand. Someone had left a few flowers on one of the stones. I stood among them, noticing.

There was a large quartz stone quite different from the other granite ones, and there was also an orientation toward the Southwest, something I'd seen already many times, in many other configurations. The circle opened on the Northeast-Southwest axis. There's a tradition that Boscawen-un is one of the more important stone constellations in Cornwall, perhaps in Britain, and even that one of the *gorsedd* or gathering of Druids took place there. I counted the stones, and noting the unusual quartz one, began to think about astronomical cycles involving the number nineteen. I thought of the metonic lunar cycle that marks the cycle of eclipses. Might there be a link between this cycle and the number and positioning of the stones? Many of the circles of Land's End had nineteen stones—perhaps they all reflected the same knowledge or tradition. Boscawen-un is also distinguished by having a single leaning stone inside the large circle. Might there be a clue in the orientation of this stone to the others, or was it a late and perhaps disconnected addition?

It is frustrating to realize just how thoroughly the lines had been cut between us and those who had raised the stones. Now the only connection, practically speaking, is our own intuition as we stand here, amid the ancient megaliths. Why were we here? What were we called to see, or to realize? I didn't know for certain, but I had the sense that I needed to be there, among the stones, to touch them, and to begin to solve the enigmas they posed, for by doing that, I was also coming to understand anew the West and its archaic inheritances and meanings.

On another rainy day in Cornwall, I drove up to Bodmin Moor, and visited a stone configuration called the Hurlers. It was a windy, cold day, and the rain lashed our vehicle, and us when we parked and got out. It blew my wide-brimmed breezer oilskin hat off several times, and we sought in vain to keep our Nikon camera dry as we made our way down a trail, amid gales and rain, toward what we imagined was the collection of stone circles. The Hurlers had gotten their name, as had so many of the stone circles, from the peculiar conceit that some young people were out desecrating the Sabbath and had been turned to stone, in this case some young men who had been punished by a monotheistic god for playing a game on Sunday.

The story of the "Hurlers" is manifestly disconnected from the archaic history and meaning of the stones themselves. In fact, it is a modern Protestant imposition between us and the actual stones; it obscures their meaning. So too with the Merry Maidens, with Stanton Drew, and various others: the stones were said to be people, dancers, young folk often, whose revelry got them turned to stone. Could there be a clearer way for a dour preacher to condemn archaic Pagan festivals by implication than to come up with such edifying tales? The actual stone circles appeared to us out of the lashing rain, first one circle, then another, appearing out of the dimness and mist. The circles are arrayed on a South-Southwest axis, and the Northern ring has its tallest stones at the South-Southeast point.

Why were there several sets of rings here? I wondered as we made our way through the fog and lashing rain over saturated grassy earth, our footprints behind us filling with rainwater. Perhaps the rings entailed different mysteries for men and for women, or perhaps the new rings were needed when at some point the population grew and needed additional ritual accommodation. T. S. Eliot referred to "old stones that cannot be deciphered," and perhaps nowadays that is really true. The photographs we took of the stones are eerie, unearthly, the lens dotted with drops of water.

I spent some time among the Hurlers, and then found to a local café run by a congenial, rotund elderly man who busied himself making hot tomato soup, and chatted about the stones. "It's not well known," he said, "but in World War Two, the Americans practiced with their tanks and heavy equipment out here on the moor, and they drove about over the top of the Hurlers, knocking many of them flat. The circles are restored," he said, "but not necessarily where the original stones were." "I noticed that some of them had been broken off," I told him. "Yes, most from American machines practicing just before D-Day." Like so many we had met, he seemed indifferent about the stones themselves, and cynical about the lore of the moor, like the mysterious black cat that often appeared "right around tourist season, funnily enough."

Earlier, I had visited the "Blind Fiddler" standing stone, on his own in a field—I'd glimpsed him as a grey flash when we were driving by, then stopped and hiked back to him—and also visited the "Merry Maidens" as well as the "Pipers" across the road. The Merry Maidens, like Boscawen-un, are composed of nineteen, possibly originally eighteen granite stones, again reminding one of the lunar cycle of 18.6 years, and like the Hurlers, the Merry Maidens' name was reinterpreted as representing punishment for infringing upon the sanctity of the Sabbath—the merry maidens were said (again no doubt by a dour Protestant preacher) to have been "turned to stone" for their impertinent dancing.

Something similar must have happened with St. Michael's Mount, an island just off the coast near Penzance, which was connected to the mainland by a long footbridge periodically covered over by the tide. I walked across on a foggy grey day, the castle appearing above us and above the island's trees, an apparition of a perfect Romantic castle. The island had been named for St. Michael, in Christian times, the archangel St. Michael being the warrior champion against the forces of evil, evil often being depicted as a dragon. Hence St. Michael is often associated with dragon-slaying, and indeed, there are a number of legends both about St.

Michael's Mount in Cornwall, and Mont Saint-Michel, its sister island (also dedicated to Michael, in Brittany).

The theme of dragon-slaying goes back far in Western European tradition, and its root may be in the Revelation of St. John, wherein St. Michael is depicted as defeating the forces of evil in a battle at the end of time. St. Michael confronts a huge, red, seven-headed dragon, eventually casting it (the "ancient snake") into the abyss, sealing it for a thousand years. One has to wonder to what extent dragons represent chthonic energy, and whether there is in the stories of the killing of dragons in Cornwall and Brittany, an underlying theme of overturning the ancient Pagan traditions, marking their sacred sites as Christian. It is said that under the cathedral at Mont Saint-Michel in Brittany is a Pagan temple, and one can suspect something similar about St. Michael's Mount.

But both of these strange islands, one off the coast of Brittany, the other off the coast of Cornwall, have similar names and legends, surely an odd coincidence. Both are associated with giants. Breton legend has it that when the land was besieged by a giant who took refuge at Mont Saint-Michel, Arthur and the knight Bedivere swam to the island, clambered up the mount, and slew the giant by cutting off his head with the sword Excalibur. And as it happens, St. Michael's Mount in Cornwall was also reputed to be the refuge of a giant, and in those days had the name "Dinsul," or "Mount of the Sun." Here it was said to be Corineus, ruler of Cornwall, who took it upon himself to kill the giants, throwing the last of them, Goemagot, into the sea himself.

Saint Michael's Mount in Cornwall is actually the residence of the St. Aubyn family, but this is a relatively recent phenomenon, historically. It's said that at one time, the island was in fact in the midst of a forest, which is why tree roots were found along the shore; and there's record of an ancient flood overwhelming that region of Cornwall over a thousand years ago. The island is bedded upon granite streaked or flecked with quartz, very much like some of the standing stones we'd visited: I recognized their composition. But none of these hints from the past help explain what is meant by an ancient race of giants, or by dragons.

What do such legends mean? Perhaps they are a way of indicating, through stories, something of the disjunct between our own time and the archaic past. Perhaps "giants" are a way of describing those who belonged to an earlier Pagan time, and perhaps "dragons" reflect something of the same, becoming the enemy of the forces of Christian civilization, their significances fading away and disappearing as time went on. But still, the references to them continued as ancient lore of "giants" and "dragons" and magic in prehistory, reminding us of an era long before Christianity was in turn succeeded by scientific rationalism and consumerist modernity.

By this time, I'd visited many standing stones, on a remote moor or hidden in a field a long hike away. I was alert by now to how they stood and where, how to find them. I drove on the stonewall-lined narrow back roads of Cornwall, our car hurtling along, me on a hair trigger when we suddenly faced another car or a lorry coming at us, so I'd brake harshly at once, eek past them, and then hurtle along again. But on all our journeys, we never met anyone like those we'd met in Brittany, where in silent communion we'd find people sharing in the spirit of a dolmen or menhirs or a sacred fountain. What I felt, what I experienced, when I asked directions, when I met people at the sites in Cornwall, which was quite rare, and often when we spoke to local people about them, was that the stones were protected to some extent, but as a curiosity, and often they were perhaps resented a bit too. I was told that this or that set of stones wasn't worth visiting, or no one knew where it was, or the like. However one interprets it, it's clear there was a divide between the stones today and their archaic purposes, now lost to and rejected by most of those who inherit them. But then I went to Tintagel.

I didn't expect much of our journey to Tintagel, or Trevena, as it's known from its Cornish name. Paul Devereux had warned us of its commercialization, but I wasn't fully prepared for the tacky, amusement-park aspects of the town, with its Arthurian gewgaws, its expanses of parking lot for tourist buses. I have a photograph of me in front of the *King Arthur's Arms* tavern sign, standing, yes, with my arms in the air, and I had some bitter coffee before walking to the legendary site of King Arthur's birth on the rough Cornish coast. We followed the walking path along craggy rocks toward the ocean and a cliff, and there, I was astonished by what we saw.

I have visited many Native American and indigenous European sacred sites, so I recognized where we were, and what kind of place this was. I walked along the ruins of a castle high on the cliff overlooking the natural harbor below, and then made my way down to the edge of the sea, where a waterfall cascaded merrily along green moss-covered rocks. The waves lapped ceaselessly against the dark slate whose copper gave the water here in the harbor and along the coast its extraordinary turquoise hues, and beside us was a large circular cavern opening, now termed "Merlin's Cave." Given the rising and falling of the tide, it seemed more than dubious that Merlin had indeed once lived here below the castle, unless he was amphibian, but that wasn't the point.

Tintagel's associations with Arthur and Merlin weren't really about Arthur and Merlin. Those were later additions to a particular and extraordinary landscape that was sacred long before Romans came, that was sacred to the Celts, and that still possesses its numinous power today. The association with Merlin, Uther Pendragon, and Arthur Pendragon is a later addition that acknowledged and transmitted the significance of this exceptionally beautiful sacred site—but the site long preëxisted the later Arthurian legends. And what matters, I realized standing near the waterfall, looking out at the Atlantic to the West, is the place itself, its unique luminosity, above us the occasional scree of a seabird, before us the ceaseless rhythm of the waves, and beneath us the hard slate below the soil.

As I stood there, on the craggy stone of Tintagel, I began to see the meaning of the Arthurian mythology, which conveyed into the Christian world essential parts of the archaic Celtic tradition, including its sacred sites. It is true that there is a forlorn quality to many of the Cornish standing stones, but all the same, we felt some continuity with the remote Pagan (rural, wild) traditions of indigenous Europe, and some of that continuity is owed to the Arthurian tradition and to that ambiguous trickster wizard, Merlin. For in such figures as Merlin, and Viviane, and Morgan le Faye, and for that matter Arthur and the knights of the Round Table, and in the sacred places to which these traditions lent their names, as much in Brittany as here in Cornwall, we could see continuity with our remote and otherwise perhaps even inaccessible past.

I was invigorated just by being at Tintagel, just by standing on its high and romantic cliff. The Romantic poets did not capture every aspect of indigenous Britain or Europe, but they did capture the exaltation of the soul in wild and beautiful places, the rapture of being among crags that spire into the cerulean air above the ocean, among sea birds and raptors. This exaltation does not belong to the crowd, but to individuals, to an individual high above the ocean looking West into a raw and breathtaking natural beauty that had not lost its power in millennia, and would not lose it, because it cannot be lost so long as the land and ocean and sky endure. In such a landscape, we recognize anew what it means to be alive.

Near the end of the sojourn in Cornwall, I drove back to London, and on the journey felt that we were traveling into another world – noisy and crowded and not British at all. It was as though Britain had decided in a fit of madness to evacuate its own Britishness. In the backcountry of Cornwall, on narrow rural roads lined by stone walls built over centuries, and not for cars, one could barely get one car past another. And out on the Cornish highlands and moors, Britain, it seemed, had not changed all that much for a thousand years. But London was another world, deracinated and confused, full of machinery and artificial lights in a hazy penumbra of electronic waves and noise.

London was modernity, and in modernity, the stones were an anachronism at best, and at worst, they did not seem to exist at all, in this world of high finance and elaborate parasitism on what had been conserved from the past. In London, in the new London, what mattered was the exploitation of the world. Walking from our hotel, before I was to give a lecture that evening, we passed some exotic Italian sports car, a Lamborghini I think, parked akimbo in the middle of a London street, behind and around it honking, infuriated drivers. Its owner, a ruler of the universe, didn't have to bother with niceties; he had just stepped out of his gull-winged supercar and walked away to his meeting or afternoon coffee or whatever, leaving it in the street until he was finished. The new London was the kind of a world where this could happen; where we had come from, it couldn't.

Entering the new London, sometimes called Londonistan now, we had entered into a society that seemed entirely dissociated from all that we have been discussing. From it, myths of mysterious islands of immortality, faery kingdoms, secret kingdoms, the standing stones, all were as if they didn't exist at all. William Blake recognized this already now several centuries ago, but the modern world in the ensuring years truly had become a desolated land, where the magical connections between man and nature and the spirit world were rent asunder, and where what matters above all was the gathering of wealth and the industrial exploitation of all that we could mine, cut down, or extract. From such a viewpoint, all that we have been exploring is as if it is not.

Chapter Five

The Mountain Fastness

The mountains rise up around the Bay of Kotor like walls, sheer, verdant, hulking. Below, the waters of the bay change color, sometimes cobalt under the bright sun, sometimes inky when the thunder and rainstorms come. The grand bay or *boka*, as it is known in Montenegrin, is shaped more or less like a vast butterfly, whose azure wings are surrounded by nearly vertical rocky slopes mostly covered with green foliage. Looking up from the blue water's edge, one can see that an overland invasion from the sea into the highlands above would be impossible: who could even scale them alone? These unbroachable walls of the Dinaric Alps protected the mountain fastness beyond for many centuries.

But the coast, the beautiful coast, that is another matter. The teeming city of Budva has its red-tiled roofs of traditional houses, to be sure, yet in the wake of Yugoslavia's dissolution came more and more high-rise apartments and condominiums, many just grey cement like those of the former Soviet Union. The once placid town on the edge of the Adriatic is abuzz at night, nightclubs pounding out electronic beats, above the empty eye sockets of unfinished greyish building upon apartment and condominium building. You can see how the lapse of communism left a space in which capitalism went mad at the shoreline, and soon, it appears, there will be a housing bust just as now there is a housing boom. The dead hand of collectivism kept the region a backwater, and now its oligarchs, many from far away, seek to make it a Monte Carlo, a luxury destination for the wealthy. It feels a little mad, and I don't want to spend too much time there.

Across from Budva is a tiny island connected by a guarded land bridge, fronted by a coastal beach of tiny pea-size stones, on which are gingerly walking and lounging sunbathers. Across the guard station to the island only resort guests can pass, said to include celebrities and the wealthy even during the time of Yugoslavian communism. That island is called Sveti Stefan—Saint Steven—and is a luxury resort, a destination for those with thousands of dollars to spend on their accommodations. A remarkable example of modernized facilities in a medieval setting, it is even today a fortress village, whose origins according to local legend are amusing.

The tiny island fortress village was said to have been built when local Montenegrin warriors heard that the Turks (led by the infamous Barbarossa) had moored warships nearby during the siege of Kotor in 1539 and were away on an invasion. The Montenegrins captured the ships, moved them and plundered their riches, and from the proceeds built the island fortress from which those living there were able to protect themselves from invaders. The town was later razed, but then rebuilt, and eventually was said to serve as a pirate base in the Adriatic, for which it was undoubtedly well suited. This may not be the only time you'll hear of a connection between Montenegro and piracy, smuggling, or other illicit activities—some variants of these are said to have lasted well into the contemporary era.

Driving the serpentine coastal road back, you might glimpse, on the face of the cliff overlooking the bay's entrance, a stone-protected path upward, zig zag, to a fortress on the top crag, and then, below it, you'll see a remarkably preserved and modernized medieval town with narrow stone roads and alleys amid protecting stone ramparts. The medieval village below, with its close stone walls and protected little town squares, has been transposed into a tourist destination, filled with little shops and restaurants, while perfectly retaining its protective stone architecture. One can easily see how the Montenegrins could have defended from and retreated above, and it is hard to imagine how anyone could have overtaken the mountain stronghold. But the coastal area was overrun many times over the millennia, including by the Romans, who certainly left evidence of their time here too. Contingents of Venetians, Ottomans, Austro-Hungarians, French, also held some or all of the coastline in this area over the ensuring centuries. When the ships and armies of the Ottoman Empire arrived, this was where they came. The fortress and its ramparts above on the side of the cliff bear silent witness.

The road snakes on along the edge of Kotor, through small red-tiled clusters of homes and occasional shops, past villas and magnificent vistas, on and on, further and further back along the edge of the bay's butterfly wings, until you reach the farthest shore from the sea, near the little town of Risan. When the Romans arrived, this was the Kingdom of Illyria, and the word "Illyrian" is still used to invoke the autochthonous ancestral origins of the people of the region. The area was ruled, at the time of the Roman conquest, by Teuta, queen regent of the Illyrians, who inherited a vast kingdom after her husband's death, and defiantly continued to allow her subjects to engage in piracy along the Adriatic. This finally brought down the wrath of the Romans upon her and her people. She retreated to Risan, home to the Illyrian fleet, and legend has it she ultimately threw herself from a nearby peak.

Entering Risan's red-tiled village today, the rocky walls of the surrounding mountains undoubtedly are hardly changed from what they were some two and a half millennia before. Here one finds a museum near the base of the hill, within which are the magnificent Roman mosaics said to be from a hotel or dormitories, one of which (unearthed from beneath a modern villa) features the god Hypnos, who no doubt guided the guests to a deeper slumber. Hypnos seems appropriate in this somnolent locale, as if there were a veil between this place, around which are protecting crags, and the turbulence of the world beyond. One could easily envision a Roman inn, also perhaps a bagnio or bordello. Time seems to nearly stop in Risan. There is a lazy somnific quality to the region. Locals say that if you see someone working, offer him condolences.

It was hot, and I stayed in a house above the village looking out over the bay, coming to know the area, hiking up, along, down, and up the steep hillside on the narrow trail and streets among the houses. I enjoyed visiting a cafe that fronts this backwater of the Adriatic, sitting near the windows and watching the light shimmer on the blue water. But eventually I drove around the edge of the bay, driving back into time or perhaps into timelessness. The photographs I'd seen showed a weathered handmade sign indicating the direction of Lipci, and an ancient petroglyph site, but no such sign was visible any more. Instead, there was only a place that looked vaguely familiar, a bus stop, and an ascending road.

Having parked the car, I got out and looked about, but saw no clear direction. There were various folks standing around, some children, but no one spoke English, and we had no idea where to go. Then, down the hill came a hiker, a robust brown-haired German with an air of mild disgruntlement, who announced he could not find the petroglyphs and marched off, his backpack moving up and down rhythmically as he purposefully strode away. But an elderly man with a staff and a kindly demeanor escorted his grandchildren to a bus, waited patiently, and when they got aboard, pointed, and began to walk.

We trudged up the street, the sun blazing down, the heat surrounding us, almost pressing into us, up and to the left, where a stony trail led from the residential neighborhood into the trees and brush, up and up. The elderly guide, his eyes twinkling a little with amusement, stayed right with us as we made our way over the stones, up, and then finally to the left. He spoke in Montenegrin, and we replied in English. Neither of us understood anything the other said, and we all smiled nonetheless in mutual recognition. We understood each other without words. And there, just above us as we paused, we could see it: the cave and above it, the sheer rock whose face bore petroglyphs many millennia old.

I had seen petroglyphs like these before. Some years ago, my father and I had driven out across New Mexico for hours to a Native American petroglyph site along a ridge that looked out over the White Sands. Compared to the profusion of Indian petroglyphs among which we had walked half a world away, these glyphs in Montenegro were fewer and far older. These petroglyphs are northwest of Risan (Rhisome) the ancient Illyrian town, and face southeast. Here you could see a hunter on a horse, stags with great horns, and what looks to be at least one doe, as well as a squared geometric figure vaguely resembling a swastika. Down below the sun-dappled rocks is a small stone cave with a rock wall stacked below the overhang like a bar, to one end a flat stone surface, above which is a petroglyph cross in a circle, or sun-cross. It looks much like an ancient barbecue, fitting rather well with the hunting petroglyphs above it. Astonishingly, given that the busy high-rise city of Budva was a handful of miles away, we were standing in the Neolithic.

But we also were standing in the archaic. We think of the archaic only as the past, but this is not really accurate. It's true that these petroglyphs are archaic, but the word here means above or beyond time. Petroglyphs are archetypal images; they belong not only only to the physical world, but also to the realm of human creation. When, standing in the same place as an ancient European stood so many millennia ago, we are invisible linked by the place itself and by the conceiver and perceiver of the same images in that place. A location like this on a mountainside, overlooking water, with a particular directional orientation, is numinous. Seneca, in his forty-first letter to his friend Lucilius, wrote of the primeval forest, of a cave, of mighty rivers and hidden springs or dark water of immeasurable depth, all known as sacred because there "your soul will be deeply moved by a certain intimation of the existence of god [*reli-*

gionis suspicion pecutiet]." And all the characteristics he mentions are here, in this ancient place on a mountain above deep waters.

We are considering primordiality. Such a place the ancients referred to as having and being a *genius loci*, a unique location with an ensemble of characteristics that, together, form a peculiar unity that we enter and with which we engage in a kind of timeless dialogue. We are present in such a numinous place, but it is also thus present in us. Our engagement with it is transmutational; we are changed by being in it. All this the ancients referred to as *genius loci*, the spirit of the place. It is present, and timeless; in it, we are in communication with the people whose creative spirit brought the glyphs into being, and with the invisible archaic realm of images that their creation manifests in this special location that has remained now just as it was for thousands of years.

We do not often think of indigenous Europe or of archaic European culture. For we moderns, only modernity seems to count; the past for us seems to be gone. And for most of us, there seem to be no invisible dimensions to anything, only the flat reality of the material world. But these petroglyphs mark this unique place as *numen*, as home to the sublime, uncanny, profound. In it, we encounter not only what we see, but also what we may not see but also is present, and this is why, no doubt, it has remained untouched now for millennia, protected by its numinosity.

Widening our scope, we might see not only this unique point along the Montenegrin coast, but Montenegro and perhaps the Balkans more broadly as possessing a special numinosity. The word *numen* doesn't only mean "good"; it can be understood as "powerful," or "tremendous," as having dimensions not only of the luminous but also of the tenebrous, not only of the sky, but also of the water and of the underworld, all the resonances of the uncanny, that which reaches us in deep and sometimes even unnerving ways. Exactly this uncanniness marks the revelation of the supernatural, of the *mysterium tremendosum* that may be experienced by being in such a locale.

If we were to scale the steep mountain crags around the edge of Kotor, on the other side we would find forests and mountainous terrain for miles, until we reach a ring of mountains within which is an imposing monastery, the main entrance guarded by a burly, bearded man in black slacks and shirt. Below the monastery is a grey stone fortress building made of stone blocks, heavy wooden shutters covering its windows, with long protective walls and squat defensive towers at the corners. This low, wide redoubt, with its formidable towers at the ends of stone walls, was the home and headquarters of Petar Njegos (1813-1851), a bishop, king of Montenegro, and the country's greatest lyric poet. Njegos was above all a warrior and a leader of warrior clans.

Inside the long halls of Njegos's fortress is now a museum dedicated to him and his historical context and lineage. Walking through its arched entryway, one finds inside, in an incredibly long series of connected rooms, traditional Montenegrin clothing, weapons, all the accoutrements of the warrior king who continued his little mountain kingdom's history of holding off the Ottoman Empire. Njegos was a tall, broad-shouldered man, whose dark-bearded likeness is found in the connected rooms of his fortress. He and his fellow Montenegrins—still today on average among the tallest people in the world—undoubtedly were formidable to the jannissary troops of the Ottomans.

Njegos is most well known within his country for his poem *The Mountain Wreath*, which celebrates and exhorts Montenegrins holding at bay the invading hordes that were able to overpower some Eastern European lands. It was not clear to me until we stood on the very ground Njegos himself had walked and defended, in the city of Cetinje, that the poem's title refers to the geography of this ancient Montenegrin mountain stronghold. For the city is encircled entirely by a ring of mountains, the wreath of mountains that made overruling the city such a challenge. It is true that the Muslims did capture Cetinje on more than one occasion even during Njegos's life. But they did not hold it, still less the mountain lands defended by the fierce men of Montenegro.

To the contemporary reader, Njegos's celebration of his people's independence and heroism may seem more than a little politically incorrect. In *The Mountain Wreath*, he extols Montenegrin heroes and excoriates those few who betrayed the Montenegrin people for their own advantage, but his greatest contempt is reserved for the invading Muslim armies. In Njegos's work we see complete certitude about the meaning and intrinsic value of his own people and their claim to their indigenous land, as well as the greatest possible contempt for the invading armies of the Ottoman Empire, whose men are identified as the spawn of Satan, as the Manichean opposite to all that is good and true and beautiful. For Njegos, the invading Muslims are not only his people's foe, but also in a metaphysical sense, their Foe.

Perhaps you think such a metaphysical opposition is overstated, but in fact, it is the leitmotif of Njegos's work. Inarguably, his greatest poetic achievement was the epic poem *Rays of the Microcosm*, a grand Dantesque work presented in cantos, whose chief religious characteristic is the unmistakeable presence of ancient Gnosticism, Hermeticism, Bogomilism, and arguably, Manichaeism. Njegos's *Rays of the Microcosm* is shot through with references to the opposition between darkness, materiality, and mortal suffering on the one hand, and light on the other. When I first read about Njegos's imputed Bogomilian streak, I confess I was doubtful. How was it possible that ancient Gnostic heresy could manifest itself in nineteenth-century Eastern Europe? It seemed to me at the time unlikely.

And yet. At first, Njegos's poem seems to convey conventional Christianity—his models were Dante and Milton, and Njegos himself was an Orthodox bishop, trained in a regional monastery as well as in Moscow. He was certainly intimately familiar with traditional Orthodox theology, and of course Orthodoxy has its mysticism of light, its angels, its rejection of worldliness, its awareness of the tragic and suffering nature of man. Montenegrins were familiar with all of these. And it is not that Njegos's poem is inconsonant with Orthodoxy—rather, it is that it can be understood to include other traditions as well, much more ancient ones. Njegos's own Serbian-Montenegrin values were those of ancient Greece, of heroism and valor.

Njegos, throughout *Rays of the Microcosm*, extols the spark of light in man, despite all man's faults, and although he recognizes the deeply tragic fate of Serbia, and the darkness in the world, still, he says, there remain streaming "holy rays of light" that guide the poet. He writes at length, especially in the first canto, about the "spark that is divine" and that rises from the "dark, dire realm" of materiality on gleaming wings, as it rises becoming incandescent immortal flame. Of course we have heard this before, in the ancient Greeks, most notably Plato, and before Plato, in the Mysteries, including the

Orphic mysteries that came to ancient Greece from the north, that is, from Thrace, and above Thrace were and are the Balkans. So too the Balkans later were home to Bogomils, who conveyed in the medieval period into Njegos's region variants of Gnosticism and perhaps Hermetism.

Now we know for sure the heterodox Bogomils had a presence in the Balkans and for that matter across Eastern Europe. But this was many centuries before the time of Njegos who, in the span of history, is really quite recent. What was the means of transmission from the medieval era to the modern? Several possibilities come to mind, the first being that the Bogomils wrote manuscripts that were stored in monastic libraries, or in a fortress or other protected place, for the better part of a millennia. That is possible, for after all, the Nag Hammadi library of Gnostic texts was found in 1945, nearly two millennia since it was secreted away. And we know Njegos, after all a bishop, studied in and had access to monastic collections both in Montenegro and in Russia. Certainly he might have come across just such works.

Of course, there is another possibility as well: oral transmission. It is possible that, in monasteries for instance, there might have been one who knew and conveyed to a promising member of the next generation indications of the Bogomilian-Manichaean religion of light. And in turn that individual conveyed the same to another, whether there were texts or not.

What's more, it is possible that such a perspective continued outside monastic institutions, in the general populace. After all, variants of Gnosticism, Manichaeism, and Hermetism as well as indigenous Orphism certainly existed in the penumbra of Greece in late antiquity, undoubtedly spread into the Balkans or originating there, as the case may be. Is it so hard to believe that some traces of them continued into the modern era, here and there?

We might recall that such an oral continuity of secret Gnostic-Bogomilian tradition from late antiquity to their own time was precisely what Bulgarian sages Mikhail Aïvanhov and Peter Deunov said they represented in the twentieth century. Who is to say they were wrong? For the existence of Njegos's great poem is itself testimony that somehow, whether we like it or not, a religion of light was visible in the tiny Balkan land now called Montenegro, in the city Cetinje, like an island in the ring of mountains Njegos called a wreath. If the ancient religion of light is there in the Balkans, and clearly it is, then it might well have been found elsewhere also in Eastern Europe. One wonders what else might be found there.

What would Njegos have thought of twenty-first century Western Europe, welcoming in those very ancestral enemies who had besieged his little town of Cetinje, against whom he and his clan leaders fought so heroically, and whom he so fiercely scorned in his epic poem *The Mountain Wreath*, which celebrated the protection of his people's ancient culture against those who would subjugate and destroy it? In a mysterious way, Njegos stirs us even today. Somehow, this warrior chieftain and Orthodox bishop in a remote mountain-ringed city protected by sea-cliffs was able to assemble a library of the works of Western culture, Greek and Roman, yes, and also English and French and German and Italian, and was able to weave it into his own distinctive work that celebrated also Serbian heroism and the ancient religion of light that was in no way in conflict with the Christian religion of light. Would he have accepted for an instant the abdication of all this? Somehow I do not think so.

It was said that the regional Muslim warlord Ali Pasha, who resided in Mostar, kept there a tower adorned with the severed heads of rebellious and piratical Montenegrin warriors. This of course was meant to intimidate them, but in fact inspired them to erect their own tower in Centinje, correspondingly adorned with the severed heads of Muslim warriors. When British visitor John Wilkinson visited both Mostar and Cetinje in 1844, he observed the Montenegrin's stinking tower with its heads, some of which had fallen off and become the tug-toys of dogs. He asked Njegos why he didn't bury the heads and stop adorning the tower with new ones. "Because," Njegos wearily replied, "then the Ottomans wouldn't respect us." A grotesque story, to be sure, but one that indicates clearly just how far from delicate contemporary sensibilities a man like Njegos actually was. He would do whatever he felt he had to in order to protect his people and their culture, however disagreeable.

Since we know now what is inside the island of Njegos, perhaps we should reflect for a moment on what is outside it. To a contemporary eye, Njegos's anti-Ottoman-empire rhetoric and actions appears decidedly out of favor. After all, don't all right-thinking globalist moderns approve of open borders and letting in invaders, not fighting them? Indeed, such individuals apparently think, we should offer the entire world's population social support at our citizens' expense, should we not? Njegos's fierce opposition to "Satan's hordes," his swords and daggers, his pistols and rifles, all of which saw use in battle, seem somehow indelicate to those who deplore all violence. But, Njegos no doubt would ask, would then they allow in those who would rape, pillage, and destroy all held sacred? There is a well-known folktale about a venomous serpent asking to be brought across a river in a canoe. "Will you bite me if I let you in?" asked the canoer. "No, no," said the serpent reassuringly. And so the canoer let the serpent ride with him, but halfway across, the serpent bit the canoeing ferryman. As he swooned and began to die, the canoer protested: "but you said you'd not bite me if I gave you a ride." The serpent replied: "Biting you is in my nature, and you knew my nature when you let me aboard."

Njegos's epic poem *Rays of the Microcosm* may give us a different perspective on the nature of those whom he recognizes as enemies of his people and his people's culture. His poem is esoteric, in that it has inner and outer dimensions. Exoterically, it can be read as symbolically affirming Montenegrin and perhaps pan-Serbian identity, but esoterically, it is clearly woven from the threads of ancient Greek and Pagan cultures, as well as of an esoteric religion of light belonging at least to some extent to the larger current of Gnosticism, Manichaeism, and Bogomilism. These esoteric aspects of the poem make it distinctive, indeed, unique in world literature. We could understand Njegos's celebration of the warriors and their heroic ethos in *The Mountain Wreath* as the exoteric protection by the sword of the esoteric traditions conveyed in *Rays of the Microcosm*, a religion of light that is at the center of the ancient cultural traditions of Eastern Europe and its forbidding mountains and dark forests.

What is more, against what were the Montenegrins defending themselves? Was it against Sufis and mystics like those who settled and emerged in Bosnia later? No—it was rather against the janissaries of the imperial subjugators, those who sought to establish an exoteric empire based in a literal interpretation of their monotheistic religion. Is that really so different than the exoteric literalism of anti-spiritual modernists of all stripes, for whom all that matters is that which can be grasped with the hands, as Plato once put it? Perhaps in the recent history of this little mountain-ringed city and this little mountain realm, we could learn more than a little that would be of benefit to us. But we might need to give up some of our preconceptions, to understand reality in new and perhaps even uncomfortable ways. Perhaps we would even need to consider such ponderables as rough warriorship, heroism, and their relationship to our culture and its greatest cultural achievements. Such awkward and displeasing questions are raised by a great personality!

Chapter Six

Know Yourself

The words *Gnothi Seauton*–know yourself—were said to have been inscribed about the pronaos to the Temple of Apollo at Delphi, the home of the *omphalos*, the navel-stone of the ancient world. There, the oracle gave gnomic prophesies. Much has been written under the sign of these two words, which can be traced throughout the ancient world and all the way to our present day. Some, ridiculously, inveigh against the very idea of knowing oneself; others use the injunction as a kind of foil for whatever agenda they might have; and only occasionally are the words invoked to imply knowledge of who we really are, which is also knowledge of the gods. But it is in this last sense that we will explore now under the sign of this inscription—and our exploration will take us from ancient Greece to Pagan Ireland.

Here I am invoking this ancient inscription to know yourself not in the full range of its implications, but for one meaning in particular: that we retrieve and come to know our own deeper inheritances from great antiquity, especially those manifested in stone. Standing before the great columns of a Greek temple, standing before the remains of an ancient Roman Mithraic temple, standing before a stone necropolis of mysterious *stecak* in the Balkan mountains, standing before an ancient passageway cairn at the top of an Irish mountain, we are standing before our collective Western cultural inheritance from antiquity writ in stone. But what does it mean? What is the relationship between me, as a contemporary individual in a technological and industrial age, and these stones placed here, in this precise location, perhaps even millennia ago? How do we know ourselves in relation to what is inscribed in stone in so distant an age?

The American essayist and poet Ralph Waldo Emerson wrote in a poem he entitled "Gnothi Seauton" that the divine is within us, but we do not recognize it:

> This is the reason why thou dost recognize
> Things now first revealed,
> Because in thee resides
> The Spirit that lives in all;
> And thou canst learn the laws of nature
> Because its author is latent in thy breast.

Emerson's language is stiltedly Biblical, but the underlying implication is clear: to know oneself is also to know God, or the divine. The divine cannot be understood via any external means; we can only understand the divine because it is within us:

All these thou must find
Within thy single mind,
Or never find.

Emerson understood that meaning is never found external to ourselves; meaning emerges only from our relationship with what is beyond us and yet also in us. "I" as subject stand before an ancient passageway cairn, an object, and it has meaning for me only to the extent that there is a relationship between my inner life and the outer world. The ancient *omphalos* has power in relation to us, as we experience it. If we don't experience it, if we aren't open to it, it is only an object. But if we are open in this special way, it is not only an object; it, and its ancient meaning and power, are alive in us.

I first came to recognize this when we visited Samothraki, the Greek island home of a Mystery tradition that long predated Greece and the Greeks, and that lasted into the Roman era. It had been a beautiful temple complex overlooking the Aegean Sea, featuring an initiatory center, a theater, a food and dining area, and of it all, not a stone was left standing after the lapse of millennia. And yet, there is something alive about this sacred place; for some visitors, the very stones sing of the ancient Mysteries. In such a place, the power of the ancient gods is indeed present, at least for those in whom it resonates. It was there that I realized there are places that have both visible and invisible dimensions, and from that realization came the book *Entering the Mysteries*. In Greece, I realized, the ancient Gods are still present behind the scenes.

Another such place is Ireland. When we arrived in Ireland, it was aboard a ship that passed over the unfathomably dark sea past Scotland. The ship was one of those great beasts whose motors hummed somewhere below, and whose vast size gave one the impression that the huge dreadnaught was truly above the waters. Down below, one could see the dark depths and still knew that they were beyond our reckoning. One could see why the ancients felt there were deities and other beings in and near the vast watery abyss. Above, grey clouds and ahead, mist.

W. B. Yeats said that in Ireland, the veil between this world and the otherworld was thinner than in other places. It is. But it takes a certain sensibility to experience this, and I don't think everyone does. We have traveled and stayed in Ireland not as tourists, but as explorers, seeking out the high cairns and the megaliths and the bullaun stones, the myths and legends that surround them, and the ways that the landscape, the stones, and the myths are interwoven. For many Irish, as for many travelers, these do not really exist; they are like phantoms of which one might be dimly aware, but that have no significance in the modern era of entertainment devices and swift travel between noisy cities.

I drove the Skoda up into the hills so we could park and hike to the high lake of *Slieve Gullian,* where, it is said, the hero Fionn Mac Cumhaill had met a witch. The witch had dared him to enter the lake to swim, and when he did, his hair turned white and he lost his vitality. Later, his men forced her to turn him back to a young man. Standing on the shore of that pellucid water in the high country, I could well imagine the hero stepping into that cold clear lake a young man, stepping out an old one. What does such a story mean? In part, it's a parable about life itself. Each of us is like the hero who one moment is young, the next is old. But it is also a parable about the thin veil between the otherworld and this one, and about how the otherworld is dangerous, how encountering it and surviving requires caution and intelligence.

The hike, like so many in Ireland, was solitary—for to go to sacred places, even on an island with many large cities, is to go into the wild, and rarely does one see other people. Every now and then, one might encounter a solitary hiker whose back is humped with a backpack, or a couple, only now and then a family with children out for a day's sojourn. For the most part, we were alone. The lake was high atop the ancient hills, like a cyclopean eye improbably nestled there, looking up at the heavens. Gazing at it, I felt the presence of the ancient stories that made it not just a lake, but a cold, clear, living myth.

The whole of Ireland is a palimpsest of stories upon stories, myths upon myths, each of which is embedded in the landscape. Traveling to each ancient group of megaliths, each cairn at the top of a mountain, I found that there was another nearby, then another, and that each of these formed part of a larger narrative that made the landscape come alive with its self-secret narrative. By "self-secret," I mean that the myths often can be known, or at least, the relatively recent ones, but their keys in the landscape though present are not recognized by most. One has to make an effort, not only to go to a sacred place, but to find its larger story, how it is nestled in the larger hidden sacred landscape of the island.

Often, these larger stories, and even the specific associations of particular places, have been lost. How then are they to be recovered? Still, there are the sacred places themselves, mute testimony to a megalithic sacred science whose nature is not part of our modern world. This is why there are so few people who seek them out—they do not exist for many of us. Of course, there are a few that are tourist attractions: Stonehenge, Newgrange, for instance. But there are countless others, not frequented by tourists, without parking for buses, without fences and ticket booths, not even marked on maps. To those, one must make a pilgrimage and rely on whatever advice and instructions we might happen to encounter. Thus, each pilgrimage becomes our own story.

I stayed in an Irish farmhouse in the Boyne River Valley, at the end of a long, winding paved driveway lined with white fences behind which cattle grazed. Each day we would venture out to spend the day exploring the cairns high in the mountains. These cairns are collectively known as *Sliabh na Cailleach*, the "mountains of the Cailleach." I drove the little Skoda up into increasingly rugged terrain, higher, up narrow roads and two-tracks until I thought it best to park and hike. There were sheep grazing impossibly on the sides of steep hills, eyeing us askance as we walked up to the stone-pile cairn from which you can see the entire countryside spread out below, a vast green patchwork vista with a river winding through it. We were remarkably high.

The Cailleach is a very interesting phenomenon, not exactly a deity, more like a female spirit of the land. There are many stories about her woven into the Irish landscape, but the most well known is associated with the cairns at Loughcrew and the other sites together called the *Sliabh na Cailleach*. The Cailleach, it is said, was a giant hag who gathered many stones in her apron and deposited them at the top of each of these high hills, making giant leaps between them, only to fail at the last and fall to her death or, one might better say, "death." Sometimes the Cailleach is a young woman; other times she is a hag; and the clear implication is that she is an immortal beyond the limits of birth and death.

It is common to refer to these cairns high in the mountains as "tombs," but oddly, they do not seem to be associated with many graves. The word "tomb" does, however, keep many people at a little bit of distance from them, to regard them a bit askance, and perhaps that is for the best, as a little bit of fear protects them from damage. Those who damage them, it is said, are subject to a curse. I would not be surprised if this were indeed the case. At Loughcrew, there is a large stone slab called "the Hag's Chair" [the Cailleach's Chair] from which one looks out over the countryside below. The Cailleach is sometimes likened to the banshee whose eerie cry one hears in some families before a death—she is a liminal, numinous being in between life and death, the eerie spirit of the land itself.

I clambered into the cairn's chambers through the eastern opening, and there found its carved panels whose incised markings convey indications of the place and its meaning now lost, for it is five thousand years old. What does it mean to climb through the narrow passage-way, like climbing into a womb, to sit in one of the the three chambers? And why three chambers? Through the narrow passage, fit for one at a time, comes the light of the sun and moon that illuminates and redeems the giant below. They stubbornly call these "tombs," but clearly they are not that. The name is a ruse.

Sitting in the near darkness, surrounded by the vast silent weight of stones, among the ancient symbols, we ask ourselves what the purpose of such a place may have been. The ancients practiced incubation, that is, going to a sacred place and staying there, sleeping there, so that in one's dreams may come the numinous visitors from the otherworld, those who belong to this place, and who reveal themselves only to those whose inner eyes are open to their presence. The outward symbols are their marks, a kind of psychic mapping via symbols. Here, deep within the archaic stones, we are engaged in the contemplative inner life shared by those four and five millennia before; we are in the initiatory chamber of rebirth in which one stayed, perhaps overnight, perhaps longer, until one clambered out through the narrow passageway into the world to be born again.

This is truly the secret island, secret not only because few come to such a place, so far out in the boondocks, but even more because one also must be in the receptive state that allows one to experience it from deep within both it and oneself. Here, the inner meets the inner; the inner responds to being within the earth's womb. In modernity, we have forgotten and lost our deep connection to the earth and the earth's mysteries; for us, these places and what they represent are as if they were not. Ours is the world of artifice and mastery of the world as a collection of objects; but this, here in the darkness of the earth, we are again the subject being reborn, experiencing the ancient path of initiation. Initiation is the secret of the secret island.

Crawling out of the cairn, alone, for the narrow passageway will only fit one at a time, we enter again into the light of day and the relentless *sidh* wind that blows unceasingly in the high sacred places of Ireland. Why is this passageway oriented in the direction of north-northwest? What is the constellation toward which it points? Were there three chambers because three would enter at once? Or are there three chambers because these are the three phases of life, childhood, mature, and elderly? By traveling from one place to another, all sacred to the Cailleach, we begin to form a connection with her; her places become familiar to us, and we to them. That familiarity between us ushers us into a rare tribe, the tribe of those who begin to experience the myths and the mythological beings as living reality.

Of course, I would not say that experiencing these myths and mythological beings is without risk. Quite the opposite, in fact. There definitely is risk. When we enter into the initiatory world, that is, the world in which we are open to the path of inner experience, we are also entering into a sphere in which what we experience may be frightening, may even overwhelm us if we allow it to. This is the realm of the numinous, that is, of awe, of exaltation and perhaps even of terror. Modernity exists in a narrow register of what it means to be human, a small wedge of a much larger range. When we enter that larger range available to our ancient ancestors, we should be aware that it is a risky endeavor.

One grey and windy day, I decided to hike to the top of Slievanamon, the "mountain of the women," near the town of Clonmel. I parked below, thinking it would be a relatively short hike, but as we climbed, and climbed, and climbed, I began to realize that it was not merely a stroll we were in for. We grew fatigued; our thighs began to hurt just a bit, those front muscles, as we walked up, to the top of the first hill, which showed us a vista from which we could see that we were only on a knoll, ahead of us another rise to another knoll. A young man in a running suit trotted past us up the hill; it wasn't uncommon to find runners here, since this was the hill up which women raced in order to become the bride of Fionn Mac Cumhaill. As it happened, Fionn was in love with Grainn, and had shown her a shortcut, so she won the race and became his wife, crowned at the top of Slievanamon.

At the top of Slievanamon, the wind howled, and I approached the cairn at the pinnacle, with its passageway open to the East. The passage had been closed by fallen stones, but here, with the *sidh* wind lashing at us, was said to be another entrance to the faery kingdom. Around us is a grand vista, a valley spread out below, and to one side, a phallic quartz *menhir* very similar to the one we'd seen at the Hill of Tara. This one leaned because of standing water near it, but still stood, a meeting point for warriors, chieftains, nobility. Within the cairn I glimpsed in imaginal vision who was there, and what she looked like. Above, the wind sang, but below, in the underworld, it was still.

What does it mean, this idea of an entrance to the faery land? R. J. Stewart, a longtime explorer of such realms, describes entering the faery kingdom as entering into an initiatory underworld. In this he followed the Rev. Robert Kirk, who had investigated the Celtic faery tradition in Scotland, and who, legend has it, still dwells in the faery land. Kirk had written *Secret Commonwealth of Elves, Fauns, and Fairies* in 1691, and in it described the faery realms as told to him by "men of second sight." Kirk writes of this subterranean realm's inhabitants that the "*Siths*, or FAIRIES, they call *Sleagh Maith*, or the Good People ... are said to be of a middle Nature betwixt Man and Angel, as were Dæmons thought to be of old; of intelligent fluidious Spirits, and light changable Bodies, (lyke thoſe called Aſtral,) ſomewhat of the Nature of a condenſed Cloud, and beſt ſeen in Twilight."

An entrance into the realm of faery happens, Stewart tells us, first through our own inner perception. But it is, he and Kirk make clear, not just a matter of our own imagination. Our imaginal faculty allows us to perceive and to participate in this other world. And what we experience, the landscape and the beings we encounter, have their own nature. The philosopher Schelling referred to it as the spirit world, and said it can be found within the nature around us. This is especially true of certain sacred places— sacred because they are more transparent than other places to the spiritual. Stewart describes the faery realm as "within and beneath" the nature with which we are familiar, terming it "an archetype of the natural world," "a timeless place of regeneration, beauty, and allure."

Similar realms are not found only in Celtic lands. Many people know about the popular fiction of "Shangri-la," and about the hidden kingdom of Shambhala in Tibetan Buddhist tradition. But actually in Tibetan tradition there are said to be numerous hidden lands, for instance, sacred valleys called *beyul*, refuges that are protected by natural and divine forces, and in which spirituality manifests naturally. These are hidden places where the powers of the earth, the lords of the land and water may be more easily contacted, and in which humans can live in harmony with the natural world by recognizing and connecting with them. It's said in Tibetan tradition that when the world is damaged and there is much suffering in the era of decline, these places will be the last refuges.

However, the faery realm as described in Irish tradition is distinctive and closely linked to the sacred landscape of Ireland. The faery realm is close to the human world, understood as something like a parallel world alive with *joie de vivre*. It is the archetypal realm of nature prior to the human fall into dualism, separation, and suffering; it is not timeless, precisely speaking, but its time is far more elongated than our own, so that a short time there may be many years here. The faery realm is inside the world of nature, more accessible in certain places, and lit not with the light of sun and moon and stars, but by an inner light. It is numinous, at once light-hearted and yet a little alarming; it is not subject to our human moral constructs, like nature itself. It regenerates; it is regeneration.

These high places, cairns, faery entrances, are numinous. I drove to Carrowkeel, drove up and up the mountain valley on one two-track that led into another, through cattle and sheep gates that we closed behind us, until finally we hiked. There, atop the high hill overlooking a vast landscape, there were cairns lined up, two paired to the left, one to the right, above it a final fourth. These are initiation passageways, inside stalls with domed roofs, and in the third of these, a great space and an array of symbols, radiating suns, spirals, petals, stars. And all the passageways opened to the north-northwest, the direction marking autumn's movement into winter. To be inside, looking out through a narrow passageway's light, is to be within cosmic knowledge revealed in space.

I hiked up to Cashelkeely, up a long trail through a magical forest full of moss and crystal streams, at the top, a circle of stones with a keystone facing West. Above, a set of three stones of ascending height pointing due East, to the circle below, with others pointing to another circle. The curved stones in the Southwest aligned with the highest peak of the mountain in that direction, to the North, down below, more lakes, and in the distance, more mountains. It is a great

network of stones, stones existing in complex re-
lationships to the height and orientation of
other stones, to water, to the mountains, and of
course, to the myths and power they express.

It is difficult to explain numinous experiences in the modern world because our language
and worldview is so conditioned by dualistic
analysis. But by being with the ancient megaliths and cairns for extended periods, we begin
to recognize that there are other ways of knowing. From a materialistic perspective, megaliths
are just large stones, and cairns are a pile of
stones on a hill. But from a traditional perspective, the megaliths and cairns are charged
places, and when we are with them and open inwardly, we begin to experience them in different
ways. The key is to be open in what I term inner
space. By being fully present to the place, not
only its physical situation in the landscape, but
also the inscribed imagery and its location
within the earth as well as its archaic, timeless
dimensions, we can begin to perceive new aspects of the whole. By being in the cairn, we are
present to the place in a way that connects us
past the lapse of time, directly with those for
whom the site was/is alive.

What does it mean to go underground into a
chamber within the rocks, in such a high place?
It incorporates the symbolism of ascent and de-
scent both (one climbs to the heights of the site
and then goes into the earth). In many respects
the passageway cairn is a site that very much re-
sembles ancient Mystery sites, like those at

Eleusis and Samothrace. The ancient Mystery initiations took place in the dark, but as Apuleius tells us in the wonderful novel about the Mysteries of Isis, in this darkness "the sun shone at midnight." Such a metaphor conveys the idea that the initiates into the Mysteries experienced a different kind of light, a luminosity of consciousness that can't be described except perhaps through metaphor and simile. In the Mysteries, one was said to experience suffering and alienation, as well as rebirth and the joy of illumination that in turn is tied to one's posthumous existence. The initiate was "twice born," by virtue of passing through the underworld in the initiatory path. One is inside the cairn's chamber alone and passes out through the birth canal of the passageway into the world again— the passage cairn is very much analogous to the ancient Mysteries in its symbolism of underworld initiation and illumination.

And in the elder Irish tradition, the landscape itself is also initiatory: by moving over it, one is retracing the path of the Cailleach, not only at the individual sites, but also moving from one site to another, and down the coast to the peninsulas. The Cailleach is a creatrix and a mysterious, numinous feminine figure in Irish mythological tradition, and as I drove down through the Irish countryside, through Cork, to the palatial home overlooking the bay that I had leased for our home base, I only partly realized that we were moving through both a physical and an imaginal landscape, into the home of the Cailleach herself.

I had espresso and magnificent French pastries in a little café the next morning, and decided to travel down the Beara Peninsula toward what is said to be the Cailleach's home, the lowest point of the peninsula, where the land reached out into the Atlantic Ocean. I stopped at Uragh, an array of craggy elder standing stones, behind which was a lake and a picturesque waterfall cascading down from the hills. Alone with the stones, I communed with them and their presences. Along the coast not far away was a Tibetan Buddhist Dzogchen retreat center, about which the presiding Dzogchen teacher said that locating the center here would bless not only Ireland, but all of Western Europe. He felt it was a region of exceptional power in the land that radiated to the Western region of the continent.

Further down the peninsula, the land grew more desolate, with great stone outcroppings and an increasing *sidh* wind that blew ceaselessly, buffeting us when we were outside, buffeting the car when I was driving. I was driving not only across a peninsula, but also across a visionary landscape presided over by the Cailleach, whose home was said to be at the tip, where a small barren island was linked to the mainland only by a cable car, below which the Atlantic surf roiled and foamed against the rocks. The wind howled, and the cable car swayed from side to side. This was truly the land of the Cailleach herself, whose presence was infused into all that we saw.

That includes not only land, but also water. There is always some connection between a sacred site and water, as one finds whenever one comes upon a holy well. Some of the holy wells have dried up, perhaps as a visible sign of the times in which we live. But I came upon a holy well, down a well-traveled path along and into a valley's forested undergrowth. It was like walking back in time, by going through the narrow stonework gate that only allowed a single person at a time, turning sideways at that; we were soon walking under silent trees and among lush foliage as if it were a thousand years before. The well itself is a dark opening into the hillside from which the clear water ceaselessly flowed as from between a woman's legs, pure water emerging from the earth, eternity giving its plash into time.

This holy well had a special quality very different from the megaliths and cairns; one felt, in the still forest among bright green moss and leaves, that the divine feminine was here, unending giving from the earth's inner dark. That the place had power was evidenced by what pilgrims had left around it: votive candles and photographs of those who were ill and in need of healing, weathered photos of those who had died, a small locket hung from a branch, makeshift branch crosses tied with string, cards, small plastic bottles, pieces of faded cloth, all markers of this reticent place's manifest, invisible radiance. The pure stream of water trickled down, off to one side, then down again, disappearing into the distance. A holy well isn't sacred because someone blessed it; it is sacred because it blesses, ceaselessly and without any recompense, for that is its intrinsic nature. Tomorrow, today, and the far archaic past, all are the same for its constant giving from dark timelessness into time.

But there are also mysteries of time. One day I set out to find a bullaun stone, said to date back to the time of the Druids. As usual, I had a general idea of where the great stone might be, yet that is never quite enough. One drives down narrow back roads, hither and yon, not finding it here, not finding it there, until one thinks: that might be a good location. I parked the car, got out, and walked through the old Catholic cemetery, past the oldest part, and clambered over the high stone wall, on the other side of which, in an open field, we saw it, a broad-shouldered rock whose depths undoubtedly were much greater than what we could see above. The flat rock surface had indentations in it, within which were round, flat smaller stones. This was what was known as a "cursing stone."

A cursing stone is also a blessing stone: it depends on which way you turn the smaller stones within the larger stone's indentations. This bullaun stone was intact, much as it must have looked when there was no cemetery nearby, indeed, no Catholicism on the island, only the ancient Druid ways. Long before the time of Jesus, the stones were here; long after Christianity has faded, as already it has in the lives of the people of Western Europe, the stones will remain. Particularly those that frighten people just a little. And this was such a place. In effect, the stone's turning is reputed to determine how things unfold in the course of time. Turned one way, with the sun, they bless; turned back, against the sun, they blight. They are, like nature itself, indifferent to the outcome.

I had extraordinary dreams and other experiences during this period. As I look back now on the dreams I recorded, clearly I was in a remarkably charged psychic state—I dreamt of female Irish beings that came to visit during the night; I dreamt of a sacred wand charged with ogham symbols carved on it; I met and spoke with beings that told me their names in some cases, and that were always themselves charged with numinous power. In this numinous landscape, on the edge of this ancient and mysterious island, I was engaged in a visionary, initiatory journey, in touch with the mythopoetic living reality on the island's finger reaching out into the ocean.

It is true what they say of Ireland, that there we are closer to the otherworld; the veil truly is thinner there, if there is a veil at all. We spent nearly all our time visiting the stones and cairns, the wells and bullaun stones, the mountains and lakes and waters familiar to the Cailleach, so it is little wonder that my dreams and visions were bright, rich, kaleidoscopic. I was in two worlds at once, the mundane world and another visible through it. Yet most people I met, Irish or not, seemed to live only in the modern and mundane. The owner of a large seventeenth-century home that served as a bed and breakfast told us one morning at length about how when he was young, folks told him and his siblings about the *sidh* wind and how, when it blew, it might be best if you lay down until it passed, so you did not draw the attention of those who traveled in it. He told his stories with gusto, but also with the clear sense that the days in which one believed such things were long gone. I experienced the otherworld in this one because I was attuned to it, but I met no one else who did.

In this sense, although one is on the sacred island, one is also oneself the sacred island. What is sacred is so inasmuch as we are aware of it. For someone who sees a holy well as just H2O and dirt, there is no holy well for that individual. The same for the standing stones and the cairns that mark the entrances to the faery realm. There is no faery realm, or indeed, any mythic being or earth spirit or magic of any kind, for those who live only in a two-dimensional world of objects. If we do not have the sacred island in us, then for us there is no sacred island. This is not to say it does not exist, just that it is *as if* it does not exist for us. Gnothi Seauton.

Chapter Seven

The Island of Those Who Can See

To travel to the Isle of Harris-Lewis is to traverse the deep darkness of the sea. One has to cross over the sea trench known as "The Minch." The waves rise, and the water is terrifyingly deep green and full of swells even in good weather. Little wonder that still in the nineteenth and eighteen centuries, the local people poured libations to the god of the sea: unfathomable depths and the ancient fear of being lost in them. On the other end of the journey over those profound waters, the island slowly appears, known for centuries as the island of seers.

In his 1691 treatise *The Secret Commonwealth*, a book about the faery tradition in the isles of Britain, Robert Kirk includes a letter from Lord Tarbett to Robert Boyle, observing that in 1652 he had made an inquiry into the prevalence of the second sight in northern Scotland. He had found that while many Highlanders were said to have it, "yet far more Islanders were qualified with this Second Sight." And, he continued, "there were more of these seers in the Isles of Lewis, Harris, and Uist than in any other place." He added that "it is a trouble to most of them who are subject to it, and they would be rid of it at any rate if they could." What is more, several of those who "did see the Second Sight when in the Highlands or Isles, when transported to live in other countries, especially in America, they quite lost this quality." The second sight, it appears, is directly linked to to the islands.

Why would the Hebrides be linked to second sight? It is true that thousands of years ago, when the standing stones were raised and placed, the islands likely were populated by aspen, birch, rowan, juniper, and other trees, or so the pollen in the deep peat bogs would suggest. And even today in a few places one can find trees and brush, but for the most part the islands are desolate, one of the most windblown places on earth. Perhaps this elemental nature, the rock and earth amid crashing waves and howling wind under rainy grey skies, is exactly *why* the outer islands have been populated for time immemorial by tellers of ancient tales and by those with inner vision. A barren outward world conduces to more alert and living inner realms. After all, just as the Cailleach was said to inhabit the southwestern tip of Ireland, so too the Western Hebrides off Scotland have their corresponding invisible aspects.

The little island of Lewis-Harris is home to Scotland's most famous and elaborate megalithic complex, that of Callanish. One arrives first at the eastern standing stones—outliers to the famous main cross-shaped site—that open out to the west-southwest. In the distance, I could see the stone spires of the main array, below it the fresh lake with water deep enough for whitecaps. I hiked to the main standing stones, high and narrow, in the shape of a cross. Of course the cross was known to ancient European cultures long before Christianity came, as it is archetypal and therefore universal. At the same time, it suggests that there is no fundamental contradiction between the ancient Pagan traditions and Christianity, that the cross can belong to both at once.

The ancient stones of Callanish run in double rows toward the north from the circle in the center, with a single menhir at the heart of the array. Seen from above, the stones are like a human form with the torso and heart in the center, legs to the north, arms outspread east to west, and the head to the south. Standing in the midst of the array, high on this hill overlooking the loch and the landscape, one is struck by the magnitude of the site, and one can see why John Toland would have identified the grand monument with the Greek mythical northern land of Hyperborea, its center with the spherical temple mentioned by Diodorus Siculus. And it is true that Diodorus Siculus refers to a northern island in the region above the Celts, "beyond the point where the north winds blow," sacred to Apollo, where there is a spherical temple "adorned with many votive offerings." Is Callanish part of Hyperborea? It is certainly associated with Hyperborea in our imaginative geography.

Was the Pagan world extirpated by the Christian overlay? The very existence of Callanish and the other sites of the Isle of Harris-Lewis suggest that it was not. Scotland became known for its Calvinist severity and its rejection, on the surface at least, of the ancient "superstitious" Pagan ways. I myself grew up Calvinist, in a world in which mysticism and the mysteries had no presence. Perhaps the intensity of the Scottish occult, if we may so call it, psychologically was somehow balanced by the sternness of Calvinism. But without doubt there are signs of the ancient Pagan world's presence even today.

I drove up to St. Moluag's Church on the northern tip of the island, an early medieval church where, it is said, lunatics were brought in order to incubate there in the church and thereby be returned to sanity. The stone church sits alone back in a green sheep-pasture, not too far from it a sacred spring. But it is not on the edge of the ocean, though one might think it should be, given some of the legends about it. For those folk legends, recorded in the late seventeenth century, tell of a Pagan ritual offering in early November (Samhain) to the sea-god Shony. A local would stand to his waist in the sea and offer ale brewed from the local grain, after which locals would celebrate with singing and dancing (and there is a hint of sexual license at this time, in some accounts). Supposedly this practice was eventually ended by Presbyterian Calvinists, but the mere fact of its reputed existence in the early modern period is interesting.

And there is more. On the way to St. Moluag's, I stopped at a little wayside museum, which featured a catch of rommel from the mid-twentieth century, mostly from the time of the second world war, radios and transmitters, what appeared to have been the mid-century contents of various people's attics dropped off and put on display. But there, amongst the *bric à brac*, was an ancient worn stone figure shaped rather like a keyhole with three holes in its top part. A closer look showed that it was actually a nude man, and in the center of the torso was a clearly discernible scrotum and penis. The stone image is dated to the 900s, and is said to be of Jesus, but is it? It certainly doesn't resemble any conventional cross or Jesus image, and indeed, it found its way to this museum because it had been removed from St. Ronan's Church on the nearby island. It had been broken in half, then restored to its original shape. And it looks very much like a male equivalent of the sheela-na-gig, with a similar posture, one arm and one leg up, one down, its genitals clearly exposed.

What, you might ask, are sheela-na-gigs? The first sheela-na-gig I saw was in Oxford, England, in the Church of St. Michael at the northern gate. It had adorned the city gate, a small female figure with its right hand on its hip, its left hand down, its legs spread, its vulva clearly visible. It now is ensconced behind glass in the stairway of the church. There are different theories about the sheelas, as some colloquially refer to them, but they do manifest explicit female sexuality, often incorporated directly into Christian church architecture. And the existence of this one at the north gate prompts one to wonder if those passing under it were meant to be experiencing its Pagan blessing of fertility.

Most sheela-na-gigs are female, more or less like the one in Oxford with its vulva exposed, but not all are female. I visited St. Clement's Church in Rodel, at the southernmost tip of the Isle of Harris. It is a strange little church whose guard tower, if we may so call it, is made of the local black quartz. On the east face of the tower facing south is a sheela-na-gig, her legs spread wide with her knees high, her right arm across her torso below her breasts, and on the other side of the tower is a horizontal "lewd man" wearing what appears to be a jacket, his hands holding his erect penis with visible scrotum, his feet pointing toward the east and the mainland. The church towers were decorated with directional animal images, some of which have since been lost, while others are still visible.

Inside the chapel are reclining knights, hands on the hilts of their swords, the elders of the MacLeod clan. The church and tower overlook the ocean, far below, and it is said that for the majority of the church's history, its visitors came from the sea to visit. In the tower, on the top window facing the ocean, are piled offerings of coins and other baubles, gifts to the god of the sea or to the protector saint, as the case may be. The chapel feels for all the world like, at the end of the world, it is Pagan and chivalric Christian at once, its knights ready to rise, take up their swords, and do final battle. It is imbued with the ancient force of martial presence.

We often are given the impression, which began with the Church Fathers, that Christianity and Paganism have nothing in common, that there is only opposition, an impression fostered by some early Christian virulent anti-Pagan rhetoric and taken up again by some within Protestantism and Catholicism over the ensuing centuries. But here, in this little island off the coast of Scotland, one encounters many clues that suggest a different picture. Here, there are many indications of crossover between the ancient, Christian, and modern worlds. Perhaps this is why Harris-Lewis was known above all other places in Scotland, even the highlands, for inhabitants with second sight, for archaic living traditions of magic. The inhabitants lived in a Christian world, but even their churches had Pagan aspects for those with eyes to see. And indeed, if Christianity is understood properly as itself a mystery religion, then it is naturally in tune with the Pagan mysteries. There is no intrinsic opposition, because human capacity and experience continue regardless of the existence or absence of extrinsic religious institutions.

But the question still lingers: why were the Hebrides known for occult phenomena and traditions passed through familial lines? What is it about these islands, and in particular, the island of Harris-Lewis? One could say that the answer lies in the presence there of so many megaliths in the complex known as Callanish or Calanais. Or one could say that the answer lies in the presence of these other unusual churches and aspects of the island. Yet perhaps it is the reverse. These outward manifestations may not be as much causes as themselves results of what underlies it all. Perhaps there is an invisible dimension to the island that conduces not only to phenomena like second sight, but also to people building distinctive physical manifestations of it in stone. And why in stone? It may be that stone, ironically so densely material, is able to store and itself in turn to augment what remains literally occult for most of us moderns. If ever there was a place that exemplified a secret island, this is it. Its secrets are engraved in stone and woven into the lives of generations past and present. And yet for all that, its real nature is coy, only revealing itself now and then to those who are alert to see it.

Samuel Johnson and his friend James Boswell went on a trek through Western Scotland and the Western islands in 1773, and he remarked at length on the question of second sight among the inhabitants. Johnson said that the second sight is called in Gaelic *Taisch*, and he discusses it with an admirable neutrality of tone.

He recognized that Christianity, and in particular Protestantism, was the enemy of the folk traditions: "The Islanders of all degrees, whether of rank or understanding, universally admit [the existence of the second sight], except the Ministers, who universally deny it, and are suspected to deny it, in consequence of a system, against conviction." Johnson reflects, for his part, "that the Second Sight of the Hebrides implies only the local frequency of a power, which is nowhere totally unknown; and that where we are unable to decide by antecedent reason, we must be content to yield to the force of testimony." The second sight, so concentrated among the Hebrideans, is the faculty of seeing beyond the immediate physical world (for instance, seeing someone's death or someone's experience from afar through images, and Johnson discusses it in a chapter along with the traditions of the bards and the *senachi*, or "man of talk."

These traditions of second sight and of poetry and tale-telling are connected, though it may not seem so on the surface. All draw from the well of shared images of that which, in varying degrees, is beyond time and space. To see one's relative in America while one is in Scotland, or to see the image of a hero in battle a thousand years before—these are more related to one another than commonly thought. The tales of the bard and the story-teller, the conveying of the myths across time, told by someone who was tapping into the deep reservoir out of which the tales are drawn time and again—this is at least as mysterious as the faculty of glimpsing what is happening some distance away. One might say that the images precede both the myths and the events seen in second sight.

According to the Pythagorean-Platonic tradition, embedded within our cosmos are its archetypal sources, called sometimes in the Platonic tradition Forms or Ideas, but actually consisting in the geometric and harmonic patterns that precede and transcend what appears in the physical world. It is possible that this little island with its mysterious megalithic arrays, represents a kind of portal into this archetypal realm. Certainly as I think back to our time on the island, and to its many aspects, its strange churches with peculiar archetypal images of a nude woman and man along with archetypal animals, its warrior knights in repose in a chapel, its circle and cross-shaped megalithic complexes, its very nature as an island in the great and deep ocean, I can see how to enter such a place is to enter into just as Diodorus Siculus suggested, a temple of the mysteries.

In such a place, it is not only that one sees—it is also what is seen. These are not ultimately separate, for to see is also to recognize that which is seen, to be connected to it, to share in its nature. When we are on this secret island, we are participating in mysteries that long, long predate us, and that are awakened in us by our presence there. What is seen and what sees, what is archaic, or who is archaic—what belongs to the timeless realm—is here the same. To come to such places is to reawaken in ourselves what we have long forgotten, in the process Plato called *anamnesis*, remembering, movement from forgetfulness to renewed cognition. Rough, raw, barren, strange, the little island always is calling us home.

Chapter Eight

Secrets in Stone

Standing in the rolling waves of the impossibly blue Pacific Ocean, looking back at the shoreline, for all the world it looks like it might be the Mesozoic era, and a dinosaur might lumber into view at any moment from the verdant foliage along the shore. The sun is deeply warming, glittering on the ocean, and one can see here and there colorful birds, the quick movement of what may be a monkey among the ceiba and palm trees beyond the white sand. Standing here looking back at the edge of the jungle, in the distance the outline of a volcano whose slopes are covered in foliage, you realize: this really is a *new world*.

Along this very shoreline sailed European wooden ships centuries before. Christopher Columbus himself came ashore near here in 1502, and others included Ponce de León and Juan Vásquez de Coronado—the most famous Spanish explorers all passed this way. Standing here, one can visualize one of their ships out on the ocean arriving, white sails filled. What an extraordinary achievement, sailing with a crew so very far from home, into such strange new lands! One has to acknowledge the audaciousness of such an endeavor, akin to a ship exploring a new star system on the far side of the galaxy.

And despite the centuries that have passed since, this is still a new world for us, arrivals from a Midwestern rural and grey wintry landscape, and for those like us who find themselves standing in the azure bay amid white-foam waves, looking at the colorful shoreline illuminated the blast of golden tropical light. What do those terms mean, old world and new world? Standing amid the ruins of Delphi, the oracular center of ancient Greece, one feels the antiquity of the place, the presence of millennia upon millennia in which the ancient tales of the gods and their interactions with humans were told, the Mysteries—the presence of the gods like the sun at midnight—were experienced. By contrast, the new world is new for all who come to it, for us, too.

I flew in to the San José airport, and then clambered aboard a small, worn commuter plane that beat us with its engine and propeller noise as it rose over the city's outskirts and up over the nearby mountains. No one, flying in such a contraption, could fail to recall from time to time the occasional crashes into the side of a mountain or a volcano, the commuter plane that plowed a fiery furrow into a hillside or valley, that drove into the jungle. In fact, one of the local airlines had gone bankrupt due to a recent crash, and kept accepting reservations and cash for months thereafter, even though there were no longer any flights. We flew low over the water, banked hard over the jungle, and dropped down suddenly onto the short runway, the air and rough earth battering us to a shuddering halt. A little airstrip next to which was a small parking lot and a couple attendants: we had arrived.

Near the coast in southern Costa Rica, there is a mystery that we were on our way to investigate. The mystery is found mostly in the area of the Diquís, a word from the local Boruca language that means "grand water," hence the Spanish equivalent, Río Grande de Térraba, Térraba being the name of the plains into which the waters run from the mountain ranges. A great delta spreads out where the waters meet the Pacific, and in the mid-twentieth century the United Fruit Company cleared vast areas of jungle forest on the nearby plains in order to put in regimented banana plantations. It is too common a story: the ecological devastation in the wake of the industrial commodification of the world. There, amid the smoldering ruins of the uprooted and destroyed forest, where there had been more than forty species of trees forming the canopy, the excavators uncovered the first of the stone spheres.

The stone spheres are found throughout this region not far from the shore, some small, only a few inches across, others huge, weighing many tons. Although there is now a museum dedicated to the most famous locations where the spheres were found, in Palmar Sud, and one can come across spheres at crossroads or installed in a park, archaeologists have yet to find where or how they might have been made. There seems to be no quarry or sphere factory, nothing but the spheres themselves, large, grey, impassive. How were they created? When, exactly? Why? By and large, definitive answers elude us, and only speculations endure.

When the stone spheres were discovered, archaeologists of course came to investigate, and one of the most thorough of them was Samuel Kirkland Lothrop, who detailed his findings accompanied by hand-drawn maps. In those, he included examples of earth and stone mounds atop which were spheres, often aligned in nearly perfect rows or other formations, sometimes atop mounds. Occasionally, the stones were lined up exactly with magnetic north, other times at angles north, or roughly on an east-west axis. The banana plantations were set up in numbered grids, and Farm 4, section 23, Mound F, had stones aligned perfectly north, for instance.

I have been to countless megaliths across Western Europe, in Brittany, Cornwall, Ireland, Scotland, always along the western coasts, so I do have some general comparisons. Megaliths and sacred sites more generally are typically found on a high point, near water, with specific directional orientation, sometimes to the cycles of the moon, including the Metonic cycle of almost 19 years, sometimes aligned with the sun on specific days (for instance, the summer and winter solstice) sometimes with the rising and setting of stars or star clusters, like the Pleiades, whose setting is associated with the time of Samhain in early November, when the ancestors and otherworld is said to be more present with us in this world. All or many of these may have some relevance to the stone spheres in their original locations. But we do not know.

Some think that the great stone spheres marked the homes of leaders, perhaps chiefs or great warriors. Others have wondered if the stones might have some unknown religious significance, perhaps having a cosmological role in maintaining balanced weather cycles and ensuring fertility, natural harmony, and prosperity. The great circular stones, some of them still buried almost completely in the accumulated soil of centuries, do not resemble standing stones, or cairns, or dolmens, or any other megalithic site I've ever visited. They appear to be of another type entirely.

And of course, some enterprising souls saw fit to dynamite a sphere or two to see if there might be gold inside. One is reminded of the Protestant fanatic in England, "Stone Killer" Robinson, a local farmer who took it upon himself to irreparably damage ancient megaliths via heating and cooling them, or of the imbecile who carved his name and high school graduation date into a cliff in a remote sacred site that featured irreplaceable Native American petroglyphs. Such callous disregard seems endemic in the modern era; everywhere I have gone, even to ancient Mystery sites, tourists and locals alike look on with incomprehension.

It is not only that we no longer have the oral traditions, the myths, the legends, the rituals, the songs, the poems, the images—in short, the culture that made these spheres comprehensible. It is also that our entire modern worldview, the globalist worldview in which all places are interchangeable and exploitable, there are no sacred sites or sacred landscapes in the sense we are exploring here. The idea that we can have ancestral and spiritual connections to a place, to a landscape, to a region, the idea that all culture in this sense is indigenous and autochthonic, all such ideas seem foreign to us, or, to put it more precisely, all such ideas somehow cease to exist in our modern world.

My Native American friends by and large find themselves in the same position as those of us from the Western European diaspora. Our ancestral tradition may well be Celtic, we may even maintain in the family a few traditional terms, even practices, but for us to go more deeply into our own tradition, we have to travel to its sacred places, we have to come, slowly but surely, to deeper ways of understanding. We may engage in practices from Asian religious traditions, yoga, Buddhist meditation, or visualization, and these may help awaken the deeper aspects of our own inherent indigenous tradition.

The spheres are enigmatic to all of us more or less equally in the modern era. They are mute, inscrutable testimony to a culture now invisible to us. How do we connect with what they are? What do they convey to us? To what are they the portal? An archaeologist who doesn't want his identity revealed tells the story of how one day he was in a remote site in the Osa Peninsula at a site that included a number of stone spheres. He was working alone there in the jungle, and found himself one day disoriented, without a sense of how much time had passed, and filled with a sense of unease, compounded by the fact that his compass had begun to move inexplicably so that the direction north changed. He was much later found by his team, who were alarmed because he had disappeared, and he said that whatever had happened, he was convinced it corresponded to the mystery of the spheres.

I have experienced somewhat similar events at other sacred sites, notably the ruins of the Mystery complex at Samothrace, which is aligned with magnetic north. I too have seen the compass needle swing wildly (sometimes a digital needle on a cellphone). Samothracians in fact commemorated an initiation into the Mysteries with an initiate's ring charged magnetically, as I discussed in *Entering the Mysteries*. There is also an alignment to magnetic north at some sacred sites in Western Europe I've been to, and indeed the Costa Rican spheres were sometimes found in an exact alignment with magnetic north. Often these magnetic anomalies might be explained by magnetically charged minerals in the stones, and the stone spheres are typically a form of basalt, an igneous, iron-rich rock formation that makes up much of the earth's oceanic crust. It is possible that the stones have a magnetic aspect.

But there is more. The spheres do have something unusual hidden in them, but it is not gold. It is, rather, something more intangible. The archaeologist who remarked on the unusual phenomena around the spheres in the Osa jungle site in Costa Rica also said he experienced time dilation and inner disorientation. Both of these are subjective, but of course, one has to add that the entire tradition of the humanities, including literature and religion, also is based not in materialism but in more intangible, inner aspects of experience. That does not invalidate such experiences, it merely is to point out that they are of a different order. There are those who think that the spheres are the products of aliens arriving in "Unidentified Flying Objects," and while I would not endorse such a theory, it does suggest something of a different order as well.

It may well be that the spheres correspond to stars. There are multiple ways to understand this, but one is that the stones may have been arranged, as megaliths from Western Europe to Asia are, in alignment with celestial phenomena, the rising or setting of the sun or the moon on certain days, the location of constellations (for instance, the Pleiades) at certain times of the year. Seen in this light, the spheres could be understood as reproducing on earth the celestial harmonies, thus reinforcing and maintaining the cycles of life. This would also correspond with the persistent tradition that the spheres were associated with the homes of chieftains or other leaders, political or spiritual—in this way, the earthly and the celestial would be interwoven.

At the same time, this wouldn't explain the uncanny phenomena that our archaeologist reported. For that, one would have to look to nonphysical dimensions. Is it possible that the spheres bear within them an intangible but powerful center that in some mysterious way embodies and manifests space and the stars? That belongs not entirely to the physical and temporal worlds that we're familiar with? Perhaps the spheres, like all megaliths, have an aspect that is not subject to time and space the way we ordinarily think of them. Such an idea might be misconstrued as "concealing gold," but the gold is of a different order entirely. The spheres, like the megaliths of Western Europe, are regarded with a little unease, a sense that the damage or move them is to court disaster.

I stood in front of the great sphere, perched aboveground among many others in an urban park. Without doubt the stones had been moved here with earthmoving equipment after they were dug up by the banana corporation employees. I strolled among them, noticing their weathered faces, their distinctiveness, and their peculiar combination of earthliness (they were excavated from the earth, after all) and unearthliness as nearly perfect spheres. What does one experience touching them with an open mind? What do they awaken in us? It is certainly possible that the stones paradoxically bear within them the vastness of space itself, globes upon the globe, among other globes in space.

It is not so well known, but in the grail tradition of Western Europe, the grail is not a chalice but a stone or gem, referred to in *Parzival* by Wolfram von Eschenbach as the "grailstone." The grailstone is termed by the hermit Trevrizent as *lapsit exillis*, which could be a form of *lapis ex caelis*, or stone from heaven. In fact, in the Parzival narrative, the grailstone is specifically linked to paradise, and is explicitly referred to as "perfection of paradise." The stone is quite mysterious—it is said to provide food and drink, and the names of those who are affiliated with it by destiny appear in a disappearing scroll across its top. There are grail maidens who attend to it, and they must be pure, like Repanse de Schoye. It is said to be clear, pellucid, and—described after mention of the Pagan Flegetanis who wrote about astrology of the planets and stars as well as the marvels of the grail—is specifically tied to the stars. Is the grailstone also a meteor?

I mention the grailstone because it is so suggestive of the idea we're exploring here, that stone can evoke not only earth or earthliness because of its density, but also unearthliness. It is, of course, strange for us to think of the grail as a stone, since we're so accustomed to imagining it as a chalice, but stone is actually much more paradoxical. A stone that embodies spiritual dimensions, that belongs not only to this world but perhaps to the stars, that is dense and heavy yet contains invisible dimensions that bring about the transcendence of the laws of time and space and that belong to "the perfection of paradise," such ideas are very evocative in the context of these mysterious stone spheres of Costa Rica.

And of course Costa Rica itself is at once a new world and archaic, home to extraordinary biological diversity. At night, all manner of strange sounds, a peculiar air raid siren howl, and the sound of fluorescent frogs calling, one of which deposited itself calmly on our second floor veranda, watching us impassively with a black opalescent eye. Near the kitchen, a huge spider crossed the floor. Was it poisonous? Perhaps. Driving from one of the picturesque azure bays, we stopped and watched a caracara bird, a black and white falcon with yellow legs and an orange band near its beak, land and watch us.

Outside Ojochal, I drove up into the jungle and ate a late lunch at one of the strangest restaurants imaginable, a haphazard affair built of jungle wood nailed together higgledy-piggledy, with daylight showing in the roof, wiring run from hither to yon, and all around the contraption, the sound of running water, even directly underneath it. Nearby was a huge three-hundred-year-old ceiba tree, sacred to the Mayan, this one so gigantic that one could use a crevice in its base as a tool shed. One can begin to believe that this enormous Arbol de la Vida is both a vast physical tree, and an image of the great tree of the cosmos.

There is a folk tradition that the stone spheres were hurled by a deity to stop storms, and the drenching rains and jungle storms are indeed dramatic and might well call for such a means of stopping them. Such a myth brings together the physical object, nature, the human world, and the divine via their magical interaction; to hear it brings us into a world in which all these realms intermingle. The key is the myth, the human narrative that re-enacts the primordial union of inner and outer, of the natural, the human, and the divine. In our world of technological power, all these are seen as divided from one another, discrete, and mythical narratives, even those of our own inherited culture, may seem childish or opaque. But if we engage them, if we enter into the sphere of the myth, we automatically begin to see the world anew.

This return to primordiality beckons in Costa Rica. Walking along the white sand shore, standing in the azure waters, hearing the strange birds, amphibians, animals, insects, the riot of sounds and scents, everything illuminated by that exceptional white-golden light, one is really in a new world. One is closer to the beginning of the world, indeed, of the cosmos.

That intimacy with the primordial is one way of describing what is present in the stone spheres, what they intimate to us. It is true that the bulldozers razed the jungle with implacable metal blades atop clanking metal treads; it is true that the modern world is here, too. I am not denying the encroachment of modernity even in such a place. But incredible fecundity is everywhere present, and connected to the mystery of the stone spheres, close-mouthed and inscrutable now and to the end of time. If time has a beginning and an end, perhaps we can glimpse something of it here, a primordial place closer to the timelessness out of which time itself appears, still another secret island.

Chapter Nine

The Cloud-hidden Island

It was not quite the rainy season, but as we hiked up the mountain trail, the rain continued to fall. The air was so humid that it was like hiking in steam, but up we went, my taxi driver interpreter and I, toward the Taoist cave temple up in the misty heights, surrounded by green jungle foliage. We arrived there in mid-afternoon, and made our way inside. Just beyond the temple, a waterfall cascaded ceaselessly, a rainbow spray in the air. My interpreter told me about the temple and its history, its connections to his family, the history of the island in this area, and much else. We were high above the sprawling city, in the mist-shrouded heights of another secret island—Taiwan.

Taiwan, once known as Formosa, has its own distinctive history as an island, its own mythologies, its own indigenous people, and its own cultural repositories of Taoist and other religious traditions. At least some of that history was reflected in this cave temple where incense was burning in an altar near where we stood. I was told the cave temple as it now existed had been built here in the mid-twentieth century after Chiang Kai-shek had taken refuge in Taiwan, though the site itself had been sacred long beforehand.

I was surprised to learn that there was an indigenous Taiwanese population historically linked to many sacred sites on the island that dated back to around the same era as the indigenous European megalithic culture, over five thousand years ago. The indigenous Taiwanese, my guide said, were only a tiny sliver of the current population, around two percent, and concentrated in certain areas. He said he'd been surprised to learn that his own family included indigenous blood, but that they kept it largely secret. It wasn't that unusual, he said; there's a lot more admixture than is publicly acknowledged.

I was on the island to give a keynote lecture at an international conference hosted by the leading university, and it was interesting to be in a literary academic culture again after having moved almost exclusively to the study of religion for many years. The conference was on the European Romantic movement, and in many respects was like traveling back in time to when literature, not political ideology, mattered. Here in Taiwan, academics were debating Romanticism as an historical literary phenomenon just as we approached them in graduate school, studying literature as intrinsically of interest in itself. It was refreshing, harking back to an earlier era .

My keynote lecture was about the extraordinary British poet and author Kathleen Raine, whom I knew well, and who was, I argued, the last Romantic. Her poetry was lit from within by her love of the natural landscape that, for her, was also spiritual. And she was a steadfast affirmer of what is true for us as human beings with the ability to directly intuit the truth behind the facades of life. "Your talk was inspirational," a young graduate student told me. "My professors never talk this way."

But I slipped out when I could. A friend who had lived in Taipei for years took us around the city to hidden sacred places, to a temple redolent with centuries of incense, to a restaurant inside a tent, where the food was cooked in the back and we sat on long tables eating strange variants of seafood and hot dishes in succession, the young waitress's eyes bright with mirth at what we ate. And I undertook forays, as much as I was able to, out of the city.

On the far side of the island, in Ruisui township above the East Rift Valley on a picturesque knoll, are two megalithic pillars sometimes known as the Saoba stones, the Dancing Cranes, or more broadly as the Satokoay historical site. The two pillars are each surrounded by rings of smaller stones, and are considered to be from the Peinan neolithic culture of about five thousand years ago. There are myths about the pillars, some conveyed by the Ami, a local tribe along the eastern coast of the island. One myth is that the two stones were originally children, left behind by their family and tribe, who became stone pillars as guardians for the people in the region. Another is that the stones were originally wooden planks or stakes that eventually became stone. One pillar is nearly six meters high, the other nearly four, and they do resemble in their distinctive personalities the standing stones of Western Europe.

The legend of children, youths, or adults being turned to standing stones is also found with a number of Western European standing stone sites like the Hurlers, for instance. Initially, when I'd heard of these legends—for instance, that youths were playing a game on Sunday and were turned to stone as punishment—I thought it was simply an instance of Christian anti-Paganism, turning the ancient standing stones into an admonishment against violations of monotheistic prohibitions. And that element is no doubt there in the case of the Hurlers.

But such legends might also contain a different, more esoteric aspect. For we might consider the legend's implication that megaliths bear within them or provide continuity with particular humans as guardian spirits. R. J. Stewart wrote of how he had inner contact with such a guardian of the Dolmen du Monts Grantez on the western side of the island of Jersey. The guardian, a king of a clan thousands of years ago, had become "linked through the stones and the special structure of the dolmen and mound, which had become an Earth-power gate or amplifier for his awareness." He was "responsible for communicating 'Earth-peace' to his people." The physical structure (the stones) can be understood, Stewart continues, as place of rebirth (womb in the earth) and a portal to an eternal reality beyond the stars. The guardian can be contacted there by the initiate through vision or dream incubation.

An analogous idea of continuity from an archaic period to the present is suggested by the legends of two children being turned to stone. We don't know about other such legends, perhaps because although there were said to be many other megaliths in Taiwan about a century ago, today, there only remains, in addition to two East Rift stones, the Crescent Stone Pillar at Taidong near the Peinan cultural park. There are said to be others still hidden in the hills, for instance at Weeping Lake, but if we cannot find other instances in Taiwan, is there any broader East Asian precedent for stones being considered human or having human presences?

As a matter of fact, we can find precedent for such ideas. On the western side of Malaysia, in a region called Malacca (Melaka), there are a number of megalithic standing stone sites that in Malay are referred to as "living stones" or *batu hidup*. They are also sometimes referred to as "glittering stones" from the legend that they emit light or glitter at night. They are referred to as living because legend has it that they gradually grow in size, but also because at least some of them are directly associated with ancient elders. The megaliths are often paired, and one known as *Datuk Tua*, near Tampin, actually can be translated as "elder lord." Other megaliths are associated with the founding ancestors said to be masters of *silat*, a martial art based in inner power.

And there is still more. For in the remote jungle of Borneo, the Kelabit tribesmen were said to have maintained a megalithic culture into at least the mid-twentieth century. During the Second World War, an intrepid Englishman named Tom Harrisson parachuted into the jungle highlands of Sarawak and spent time among the headhunters of Borneo in that region, who lived in longhouses and maintained a tradition of moving, placing, erecting, and carving megaliths in their native landscape. The megaliths were linked to the dead and to the ancestors more broadly, as directed by a local shaman or communicator with the deceased. The megaliths of the Kelabit were not like contemporary gravestones, that is markers, but were more like portals between the living and the dead.

Taiwan seems strikingly bifurcated to this outsider. Moving through Taipei, there are concrete Soviet-like apartment warrens to the sky, yet in the mountains there are Taoist temples in seemingly pristine verdant nature. One the one side, the hive, on the other, the mountain sage. Ancient China is preserved here, despite it being aboriginal space. But the aborigines, whose presence is in many families, my guide tells me, are largely forgotten and ignored.

As we hiked down from a Taoist mountain cave temple, my guide (an earnest young man in his twenties with a degree in the sciences) told me about the aboriginal communities around Taiwan, where they are congregated, and a bit about their mythologies. He told me that they worshipped pots, which seemed to me a rather peculiar rendition of aboriginal mythology. There are indeed complex aboriginal mythological traditions about pottery, which is linked to all kinds of ceremonial practices, and harks back to tribal origin. The clay vessels were traditionally decorated with mythological beings like serpents or snails that symbolized clans, and the Paiwan tribal nobility emerged from a clay vessel impregnated by the sun. There are more than a dozen indigenous tribes on the island, each with its own distinctive traditions; they are the keepers of the sacred hot springs on the island. I was not surprised that the dominant society paid no heed to them, though, and I know from experience that indigenous traditions about sacred landscape are typically the most ignored of all.

My guide and I drove in the little yellow Japanese car up a winding road to a new Taoist monastery built on a knoll overlooking the valley, in the distance the edge of Taipei. It was, he said, relatively new. It looked it. We made our way past a group chanting a liturgy, and met an older man who, it turned out, had funded some of the construction cost. The temple was built on a much older sacred site, and the guide, acting as interpreter, conveyed an introduction to the place and those who were engaged in ritual there. We stood before a richly decorated, elaborately carved altar that featured the sea goddess Matsu, with her dark face, red dress, and two flanking male warrior companions, gives one that sense of nature's indifferent fury and perhaps also salvation from it.

Several days before, my friend had taken me to Ciyou Temple in downtown Taipei, which was dedicated to the goddess Matsu. But that temple with its distinctive wave-like roof, constructed in 1753, and now in a busy part of the looming concrete city around it, radiated waves of devotion and peace from the countless devotees over centuries. At night it was alive with visitors and lights—it felt very much like we were going back in time to a version of China now disappeared on the mainland, yet here very much alive. And one could sense the centuries of veneration there.

The Matsu islands are a more remote part of Formosa, with quaint villages and high mountain trails overlooking ocean vistas. The main green island reclines nearby. The island's archaic identity is as an oceanic home, surrounded by sometimes fiercely lashing waters and wind—there are reasons worship of a sea goddess is so widespread here. I would have liked to have explored the Matsu islands, to have explored Formosa itself, not its densely compacted, crowded, and noisy megalopoli, but rather, its mountains and seascapes, its islands and its secrets. I know there is far more to be found and known on this island than I will ever be privy to.

But what I do come to appreciate, in my sojourn here, is that it is a place with its own remarkable identity, and that it is under threat. That threat is partly symbolized by the looming concrete apartment warrens that one encounters wherever there is dense population, a concentrated form of modern global faceless conformity whether Eastern or Western, Northern or Southern. Uniformity and conformism without any acknowledgement of nature, this is the global hive mentality where everything is interchangeable. And Chinese Communism, with its hatred of spirituality and spiritual traditions, is surely a part of the threat to this little island. Will it survive, one wonders?

What does it mean for such a place to survive? So many of the secret islands, real and metaphorical, that I have visited and that feature in this book, are at risk. What is at risk is not the existence of the island, for the most part, so much as the existence of what is most precious and secret about it, its hidden dimensions. Those have existed for millennia, but in an era when vast militaries and bureaucracies can overrun a place, when invaders can overrun and irreparably damage a landscape, one has to wonder how endangered these hidden places are. Already Taiwan has only remnants of its aboriginal cultural inheritance; and one has only to peer over at the recent history of Tibet to see what destruction can be wrought in an historical instant.

But like the mountains hidden in the mist of clouds, the secret aspects of islands are akin to what Tibetan Buddhists refer to self-secret, for their secrets are hidden from most by their very nature *as* secrets. It's not that someone has hidden them away. Rather, even I, coming in from outside, can begin to discover them, only because I am alert to them, I know what to look for. I have the eyes to see. Not everything, of course, not like a native, but still, it is possible to recognize the signs once one has enough knowledge and experience.

Signs of what, you might ask?

Chapter Ten

Secret Hawaii

It is the largest active volcano on earth. From the ocean, you can see it: a vast expanse of cracked, jet-black lava that poured over the round of the caldera, where you can see inky spillage from the lip of the bowl, a solidified shattered pool spreading out below all the way to the sea. In between, a small area with petroglyphs, small cups, circles within circles, and figures of humans bearing messages of the invisible. Standing here, we are looking at the primordial origin of our world, which did not (as is commonly believed) only emerge once, in the distant past, but is emerging right now, before us.

Standing here, surrounded by the sulfurous breath of the deep earth rising up through the jagged crevices and holes around me on this crag from which we can see the volcano's lip, we are present at the birth of our world out of fire and brimstone, magma and mystery, the dark wrath on whose waves all the green eventually took root. Even here, so close to where the volcano erupted, there is green, even on the black lava plates, in every crack are green plants emerging, and not far from them, insects, birds, mammals. This island is perhaps the newest land on our entire planet, an Atlantis in reverse, rising up out of the ocean in all its splendid newness. O brave new world!

Although some time has lapsed since I stood overlooking the volcano's gray flanks, I could feel then and can feel still the deep red heat and lava below, in the depths of the earth and in myself. Can we really separate ourselves from our world and its origins? Perhaps the illusion is that we are separate. The dragon's warm exhalations rose, misting camera lenses and eyeglasses, the underworld breathing clouds out of the ground around us. This is sacred landscape as living presence and imminent danger. We could step into a crack and disappear, or what now appears to be solid might dissolve into the depths and fall away into reddish molten magma.

For a couple dozen miles from Kilauea's crater, the paved road runs through jagged earth and low brush, then comes out onto long black vistas of shattered black lava rock stretching toward the horizon, the platelets rising up over one another akimbo, resembling an alien planet. Then there is a vertical drop toward the Pacific Ocean, the road circling around and down to a dusty area where a few cars and trucks are parked, a few signs, and a series of rock piles marking a trail out into the barren rocky landscape.

Out there, somewhere beyond the rock pile markers, are petroglyphs. I find a few petroglyphs here, unmarked, on the other side of the road, atop lava plates, staring up at the sky. Circles with dots in the center, cup mark indentations. I meander along the trail, keeping an eye on nearby igneous rocks, up along ridges and down inclinations, from pile marker to pile, until at once I see them: circles within circles, a dot within a circle, and stick figure human forms. Here they are: Pu'u Loa petroglyphs, said to be more than twenty-three thousand of them, the most in the entire island chain.

What do these petroglyphs have to say to us, today? They speak in a primordial language of symbols, images borne from the invisible directly into stone, in this realm itself borne of petrified lava rising up out of the waters. The concentric circles, the circles with a dot in the middle, those mark the center of the world, the origin of the world, and the shape of a volcano. The human figures mark the birth of humans in this new world, born from timelessness into time in this primordial new earth. Tradition has it that a newborn's umbilicus would be put in a cupule on the petroglyphs, signifying coming into being in the beginning of the world, here, now. Insistently the petroglyphs remind us, you are here, at the primordial birth of your world.

This is the heart of the secret island, here, where the molten fiery red-black lava boils beneath the surface, and the steam rises around us from the earth's intimate caverns. From here

emerges land from the waters, the plants, insects, animals, humans, birds, all the beings of
the dizzying richness of the jungle. The center,
the dot in the middle of the circles, is the origin-
point from eternity into time, the axis at the center of the world. Culture is that which expresses
in different ways our relationship to the center.
Other sacred places exist in relation to it, and
are expressions of it too. But we start here because it is the primordial, ceaseless beginning.

But there is another point on the secret island to explore: the Pu'u o Mahuka Heiau, a sacred site overlooking Waimea Bay on northeast-
ern Oahu. This particular *heiau* is high above
the picturesque arc of white waves lapping the
sandy shore, in the distance the dazzling azures
of the Pacific. It has long, low stone walls,
stretching away and down from the platform at
the end away from the waters. One can easily
imagine the warriors filling it, at the top of the
platform the chief(s) and head warriors. It is
said also that here were conducted human sacri-
fices by the indigenous Hawaiians to ensure suc-
cess in warfare—indeed, some argue several of
Captain Vancouver's men met this fate here. A
local Hawaiian told me jocularly when he gave
me directions to it, "yes, that's where we ate
them." Not necessarily the most elegant of de-
scriptions!

It is a place from which one feels one could
launch out like a bird of prey high over the waters. This heiau is masculine, dedicated to the
god(s) of war, to the realm of power, authority,

sacrifice. And here one feels very strongly the sun, the ocean, and air: a rise high above the shimmering water, filled with golden sunshine and above the ordinary earthly world below, even as it is on and of the earth rising up to meet them. Here one feels a particular kind of mana, or living spiritual presence, one of soaring authority of the deities of the sky. To be present in such a place is to participate in its cerulean splendor, just as to stand near in the sulfurous mist of the volcano is to participate in that. It is, the secret island tells us, to participate in what it means to be primordially human in a primordial place.

And there is still another juncture on the secret island, the Kukalinoku Birth Stones, in the island's very center. Whereas the Pu'u o Mahuka Heiau is high above the ocean, the birth stones are in a very different kind of terrain from which the ocean seems very remote. You find the birth stones at the dead end of a highway T intersection, just beyond where the cars and trucks ceaselessly pass by on the traffic artery. It is a strange juxtaposition: in the one direction, the relentless noise of traffic and movement of modernity; in the other direction, rows of standing stones and then beyond, the quiet earth island of the birth stones. As you walk closer to the birth stones, the noise of modernity fades, and instead you hear birds and see green, ahead, a grove of trees marking the birth stones embedded in the earth.

The birth stones are so named because it was here, it is said, that royal women gave birth to high chiefs so that they would be born with greater mana, and in fact, these stones in the center of Oahu are also referred to as the island's *piko*, or navel. Whereas the Pu'u o Mahuka Hei-au, as a warrior site, was said to witness human sacrifice, the Kukalinoku Birth Stones were open to those who had not participated in that act, and the prohibition makes sense in that the site is home to feminine, birthing energy. Indeed, as if to underscore this, in the distance the mountains resemble the form of a reclining woman; and the stones in the grove, embedded in the earth, often have indentations in them in which rainwater collects.

Seeing these stones, being silent with them in a gentle spring Hawaiian drizzle, I was reminded of a stone that I visited in the San Francisco area. I had traveled there for another reason, but during my time there I looked, as I often do when I travel, for local sacred sites. I found this one, tucked into a valley between rows of condominiums and houses, in a little wild strip through which water still flowed out of and over the earth among trees and flowers. There was a large stone, along the top of which was an indentation like some of these here, said in oral tradition to have been made by women's hands because the stone (whose top glistened with water in the indentations too) awakened fertility in them. It was a in a valley, near a spring, and for all the world around it, was little changed from a thousand years before.

One more secret point on the island: moved to stop at a park on a sunny day, I walked along its edge, down to the far shore that looked out over the Pacific Ocean into the azure distance of the white-capped waters. There, on the hill's edge, was a cairn of large blackish stones. This was a "leaping-off point," so called because it is said in Hawaiian tradition that when someone dies, their spirit goes to this point and from here, out into the otherworld represented in the vastness of the ocean. I am reminded of the Bull Rock off the coast of Ireland, with its arched opening through which the souls of the dead were said to pass. There are a number of such leaping-off points around this island, some in hard-to-reach areas requiring a long hike, and here, unexpectedly, was one that presented itself to us unbidden!

It is interesting that rock characterizes all of these sacred sites; stone is what conveys the energy from the archaic past into the present and future. Of course there are petroglyphs at some of these sites, sometimes in profusion, but I am not referring here only to petroglyphs, a few of which are visible at some of the birth stones. Rather, I am referring to the nature of stone itself, as marker, yes, but also as conveyor or transmitter in ways that we in the modern world do not usually recognize. Sacred stones are a living synergy between a very specific landform and its geomantic significances, the archaic culture that recognized this synergy, and us now, standing here with them, perhaps even in touch with them.

The question, of course, is *how* we are in touch with them, how we come to understand them not only in superficial ways, but in the deeper ways of what in ancient island cultures is termed mana. If we turn our attention from the outward to our inward experience, can we be in touch with what is present in these archaic sacred sites? What can they awaken in us? And what of that are we prepared to receive? We are not so accustomed to alert inward observation, being so indoctrinated with external stimulation and the tyranny of external measurement, but that does not mean we cannot perceive and participate in what is, after all, available to us by virtue of being open to the archaic present as human beings.

Hawaii, as the newest land, is the ideal place for engaging with our archaic present and future—for here, all human beings are new also, in this truly new and primordial world. Even those who have been in the islands the longest are themselves new compared to the countless millennia of the Indo-Europeans in their indigenous lands. To be here and truly aware is to participate in and come to understand more deeply who and where we are in this green and living new earth. Air, water, earth, sun, moon, stars: our destiny is to rediscover what these really mean for us, on these islands on the island of earth moving through the vastness of space.

Chapter Ten

Island in an Inland Sea

For me, home is in the center of the palm of the hand that is Michigan's lower peninsula. Ask a Michigander where he's from, and you almost always will see a point indicated with a finger on the open face of the other hand. The gesture's ubiquitous in the state. Less common is the recognition that surrounding the hand is the largest body of freshwater in the world, truly an inland sea. Michigan itself is nearly, though not quite, an island resembling a hand in an inland sea. And it is certainly home to islands along its shores. What we will explore now are some of the inland islands' secrets.

When I was not long out of high school, I took to backpacking, and traveled alone to Isle Royale, a national park wilderness, home to packs of wolves, moose, and dense northern forest. It was then, and is today, the least visited American national park. In the midst of Lake Superior's cold, dark, and formidable waters, the island is said to be a wave of the world's largest lava flow more than a billion years ago. I boarded a ferry on a rainy spring day and by the time we were halfway out to the island, the waters were rising and falling with such ferocity that people around me were vomiting over the rails or scrambling for the toilets. We arrived cold, wet, under gray skies, on the remote island which has no enduring human settlements, no roads, only trails and a lodge.

An Ojibway name for the island was Menong, or Minong, and there is actually a Minong, Wisconsin, the name taken to mean the highlands. A high place, directionally oriented, near water, characterizes nearly all sacred sites that I have subsequently visited. Was Isle Royale considered sacred by American Indians? They typically were said to only visit, not live there, certainly a clue. The encampment on one end of the island is called Windigo, and that word deserves a little attention. A windigo is said to be a subset of the manitou, manitous being the spirits within nature. Certain areas are held to be especially the abode of manitou, that is, places that are full of spiritual power. But power can be manifested both as good or as bad. The windigo is bad power.

Specifically, a windigo in the Great Lakes Algonquin tradition is said to be an insatiable, cannibalistic, feral, tall, thin, preternatural creature dwelling in the deep woods. The horned, monstrous, decaying windigo emerges out of the deep forest to prey on humans, and in some lore it is said that the windigo is inwardly or originally human itself, or has a human in its center.

According to some Native traditions, the human within the windigo must be either rescued and extricated or killed for its insatiable hunting of humans to end. There is a legend that such a creature existed in the area of Roseau, Minnesota, in the late nineteenth and early twentieth century, and that it had a number of victims. But the windigo is only one of the larger category manitou.

Manitou refers to the spirits pervading the natural world, and we might remember that like nature itself, so too the manitou can be understood as not human. We humans tend to attach ourselves to this or that result, to see the natural world through our own veil of projections. But nature does not operate in that same way; the eye of the hawk looks at its prey instinctively and without mercy. So too the manitou are what they are, and do what they do as non-humans. The healing power of the sweat lodge is said to be from the manitou permeating and restoring those who participate in it. There are manitou in rocks, in the earth, in trees and animals, in the air, and water, in all of nature.

And there are certain places imbued with manitou, many of the islands, like Isle Royale, Manitoulin, and North and South Manitou near Sleeping Bear Dune. There is said to be archaeological evidence of Native people visiting Isle Royale for more than four thousand years, and human presence on Manitoulin for at least nine to ten thousand years. The very name means "cave" or "island of the spirit," the former derived from a Native tradition that there is an underwater or underworld spirit living in a cave beneath the island. Manitoulin is the largest freshwater island in the world, but it is obviously only one of many Manitou islands in the vast deep waters of the Great Lakes.

Sometimes there is a double name—the alternate being "Devil" or "Devil's" Island—but that corresponds to the double nature of the manitou legends, the fact that there are good and bad manitous, light and dark. And there is a confessional Christian interpolation here, whereby the Pagan, whether indigenous European or indigenous America, was deemed by Christian believers to be "of the devil" especially if it was traditionally sacred. In indigenous Europe, as in indigenous America, gods or spirits reflect the indifference of nature herself; the spirits or gods very well may not conform to conventional human norms; they belong to a different order.

Why are islands so often associated with the sacred, with manitou, spirit, or life force? There is the occasional Manitou Beach, but many of the Manitou names in the Great Lakes are given to islands. Perhaps it is the very nature of islands themselves, as set apart from the mainland. They naturally have the characteristics of sacred sites: they have high points, stone, often quartz, obviously they are demarcated by water, their distinctive features often have directional orientations, and they are truly Pagan in the sense of remote or distant from social centers.

One has to travel to get to them; they require a sometimes arduous pilgrimage. And they even sometimes have their own distinctive weather patterns, as if they belong to a different order than the mainland. Islands are naturally manitou; they are primeval.

To get to the island, you must cross water; you must make the journey perilous. Beneath the waters of Lake Michigan between the mainland and North and South Manitou islands, there are numerous sunken ships and boats, run aground or sunk in storms, littering the sandy bottom. Indeed, there are many ghost stories about these islands, which are said to house the lamenting spirits not only of those lost, but also of those who stood on the shore looking out to discern the fate of loved ones, anxious, disconsolate, broken-hearted. Some, it is said, still wait, looking out toward the waters' depths. In this regard, these spirit islands are similar to the remote megaliths and cairns of Ireland, Scotland, England, and Brittany: the local folk generally regard them with a bit of caution, a sense that there might be something here a little bit dangerous.

These islands are numinous. To step onto the island is to step into a sacred space demarcated from the rest of the world by the lake waters. This was perhaps expressed in the indigenous myth of the mishipeshu, the water dragon of the Great Lakes, sometimes said to be an underwater lynx or panther. The mishipeshu is linked to storms, thunder and lightning, and death and misfortune, that is, with danger. The roar of the waters is the roar of the water spirit beneath the waves. It, and water serpents, are the enemies of the Thunderbirds just as in Buddhist and Hindu tradition the nagas (water spirit beings) have as their main enemy the mythical flying garudas. To be on the island is to be in the field of the water, earth, and air spirits: one's spiritual horizon is greater in such a place. So is one's risk.

This is why from time immemorial, these Manitou islands were places of pilgrimage, not of dwelling. One doesn't dwell in the liminal realm where the spirits are closer, one goes there for a ritual purpose, and then respectfully leaves. One might engage in incubation there, sleeping on the island and watching for portentous dreams or visions. But one doesn't live there indefinitely; the voltage is too high for that. There are few if any tangible traces left of the indigenous presence on these islands off the coast of Sleeping Bear Dunes, in the deep blue waters. We no longer know what rituals were conducted there, who visited them and why, except for occasional folklore. But having been to so many sacred places elsewhere, I recognize them all the more clearly now when they are so close to home.

It's common for we moderns to think of sacred places as somewhere else, and indeed, I myself have spent many years exploring the sacred places of Western and Eastern Europe and Asia as well as of the Americas. In fact, this book is fundamentally a meditation on those explorations. Yet now, as I turn my attention to home, here in Michigan, what I have sought abroad is here too, even though I didn't have the eyes to see in the same way before. Some Tibetan Buddhist texts advise that one of the most difficult obstacles to spiritual awareness is being too busy, and for most of us, home is where we are perpetually busy, going to work, coming home from work, working, our attention always occupied. And of course our modern society instrumentalizes all that we see, even during a "vacation," where leisure occupies our time, not a pilgrimage. Who today thinks of a pilgrimage in the region where we already live?

However, we *should* think of where we live as also being home to sacred places, not only a building at the crossroads of Fifth and Main Streets, but also sacred places in the way that they are understood around the world, those distinctive landscapes that feature high points, water, directional orientation, and human interaction. And it is vital that we also recognize islands as sacred spaces, especially those islands that have been recognized as numinous from time immemorial. In fact, my entire home state of Michigan, surrounded as it is on three sides by Great Lakes, can be understood as such a place too.

Calling us from the future are new cultures developed from a renewed understanding of our ancestral and living connections to the landscapes around us. In quantum physics, there is the notion of the future affecting the present and past, a mind-bending idea that is arguably more applicable here than anywhere. Imagine new cultures integrated with sacred landscape, cultures that bring us back into alignment with the celestial and earthly rhythms of life. Perhaps such a new culture, to come into being in the future, has to begin by germinating in our own time the future that inexorably calls us toward it.

Modern technology remarkably gives us the power to fly above and to reshape the landscape around us; it appears to make us independent of space if not of time. Our huge machines, tractors and earthmovers, busses and airplanes, massive ships, all seem to give us the power to be separate from the natural world. However, that hegemony is only apparent; for within ourselves, we are inextricably linked not only to the natural world, the landscape around us, but also to the celestial rhythms that ceaselessly move within it and within us.

The ancient megaliths, attuned as they are to the hidden cycles of the moon, sun, stars, and planets, also are chthonic conduits for ancestral consciousness. By touching a megalith and standing in its ambit, we experience the standing stone itself, as well as all its invisible alignments and continuities. Each stone is unique in its characteristics and configuration, like a stone island linked to other stones and to the larger site, and beyond that to the celestial rhythms that course through it by virtue of where and what it is. That is why the ancients left their stone monuments, their petroglyphs, cairns, and standing stones: stone is metaphorically eternity's still point in moving time.

It is of course strange to think of my home state of Michigan as a sacred landscape, accustomed as we are to being told that every place is interchangeable, that we are all global "citizens" not home anywhere, and so forth, as the propaganda goes. But how could a landform in the shape of a human hand, in the midst of this vast inland ocean, *not* be a sacred landscape? To realize this is, for me, perhaps more of a surprise than it is for you, dear reader. And in fact there is more.

For I grew up on a farm in western Michigan, and as I tell the story in my book *Island Farm*, our farm was founded in the nineteenth century by our great-grandfather. He called the farm "Island Farm" because the fruit-growing land consisted in some ridges of higher ground amid the black waters of peat bogs and swampland. Our farm, then his family's farm, was a small island amid brackish dark water. And my grandfather commemorated this name by carving it into a stone that still stands just northwest of the main family farmhouse where my cousin now lives with his family.

I mention all this because in some respects it encapsulates many of the things we've been exploring not only in this chapter, but in this book as a whole. "Island" can be understood literally and metaphorically, as a geographic designation, but also as symbolic, and universal. Since we were all raised in the Dutch Calvinist tradition, notions like connections between lunar, solar, planetary, or stellar patterns in relation to the earth, water, and human ritual activities seem very remote from our prosaic working life on the farm. But those connections are there and are within each of us even if we do not at present recognize them.

Developing new cultures means recognizing those hidden connections, the invisible links between ourselves and our ancestors, ourselves and the rhythms of the earth and sky. It means revitalizing the natural harmonic balance between humans, animals, the landscape, the waters, and the celestial rhythms of life. Such a process is not artificial but itself both natural and inevitable, because what is natural will flourish, and what is not in harmony with nature in the end will not flourish. New cultures are as inevitable as nature's own rhythms.

Our life can be understood as a series of concentric circles, each one being an island nestled within a larger series of circles. For me, there is the circle of the family farm, the circle of the great lakes, the circle consisting of all the real and metaphorical islands within greater oceans that I have sojourned on, and finally the azure and white globe floating in the vast ocean of space itself. We are all on an island, and in this final chapter, we will explore the nature of that island and what surrounds and infuses it, this sphere that we call home.

Chapter Eleven

Conclusion: The Visible in the Invisible

John Pordage was an unusual fellow, by most people's reckoning. He and his small circle of fellow British practitioners in the mid-seventeenth century were Protestant theosopher contemplatives who belonged to the larger circle of those identifying with the great German mystic Jacob Böhme. Pordage lived in reclusion for much of his life, focusing on deep contemplative states and visionary experiences that he detailed in multiple books. His fellow contemplative, Jane Leade, wrote that she had known him to be in a contemplative state for up to two weeks at a time. As we will see, Pordage suggested something quite interesting about our world and our human condition within it both in this life and in the afterlife. I begin with Dr. Pordage (as he as known during his lifetime, since he also served others as a physician) because he opens a door into a very different way to understanding ourselves and our world, one that is not familiar to most of us.

In this book, we have journeyed to many different islands, both metaphorical and literal. Some are famous islands, some little-known, some symbolic, some mountainous islands of the spirit, some megalithic. All are mysterious in their own ways. But we have not thought about islands as cosmological and metaphysical in nature—such ways of thinking, like Pordage's mysticism expressed in his life's work, are foreign to us in the hectic modern world, bent as it is upon emphasizing action in the outward world. We are doers, not seers, in modernity. Pordage, by contrast, was a seer. And what do we see when we understand islands as inner phenomena?

Pordage wrote from his direct visionary experience, and his various books are essentially records of visionary revelation. Hence his *Sophia* is arranged as a series of journal entries from particular days, but all of his books reflect what Pordage understood in contemplative vision. The only one that remains in the original English, however, is his *Mystica Theologica*, available in modern English along with the original illustrations under the title *The Wisdom of John Pordage*. There, Pordage explains that what we experience as the physical or elementary world is only one world among a number of realms existing in eternal nature, which in turn emerges out of the "abyssal chaos."

Eternal nature, Pordage writes, was produced "so that all the ideas, forms, and patterns in the divine mind might become actual and substantial." In other words, "eternal nature was produced to be a medium between two extremes, God and the creature, whereby God might communicate himself to creatures, and creatures might have fellowship with him." Eternal nature in its pure state is the means of the transcendent Divine revealing itself to itself. It is the means by which the Divine may manifest itself and from the human perspective, is the conduit of divine love and the transition from the fallenness of duality and time back toward unity and self-transcendence.

Eternal nature itself can be understood as a circle with a dot in the center. The dot is the divine eye of self-cognition, existing in the space of the "abyssal nothing." Within the circle of eternal nature are six worlds comprised of different principles, for instance, the love-world of the angels, the wrathful fire-world of hell, the paradisal realm of light-fire, and the four-elementary-realm of our own visible world. But these each also may be conceived as islands or individualized realms within the space of the abyssal nothing. The various realms of existence, as well as divine self-cognition itself, the basis for all the realms, can each be seen as islands within the larger ocean of the abyssal nothing.

The act of divine-human self-cognition can be understood as the primordial island, the island of consciousness that is also a portal or transition from divided to divine self-awareness. It exists in an ocean of luminous self-aware love and loving-kindness. The idea of an island as a portal is, of course, implicit in the oft-repeated observation of W. B. Yeats that in Ireland, the veil between this world and the otherworld is thinner. And it is implicit in so much of what we have explored in this book. An island, whether metaphorical or literal, is that which rises out of the ocean and *is*. In this respect, a dolmen, a cairn, a megalith is also like an island: it is stone rising above earth.

Every island is primordial. To be on the island, or to be in the sphere of the island, is to be where the wind and the sun, the rain and the rock, the primal elements are more present and visible than anywhere else. To stand before a megalith, to stand on the edge of the island, is to be closer to timelessness, to be the primordial man or woman standing at the edge of existence in between timelessness and time, the vastness of space and the particularity of ancient stone. The secret of the island is its primordiality. Standing on it, we are standing once again and always, at the dawn of time.

Pordage's work reminds us of the metaphysical significances of the island. Fundamentally, we are each islands. Our awareness exists as an island in the larger ocean of awareness that surrounds it and in which it exists. Ultimately, our awareness is really awareness of awareness itself, consciousness coming to know itself, and in that sense the secret island is a metaphor for the miracle of how our we and our world ceaselessly come into existence out of timelessness and into time.

Every island is archaic. By this I mean that when you and I are standing together at the top of a mountain next to a cairn, we are on a symbolic island in the sea of turbulent air. So too, when we are walking along a high ridge above the White Sands in New Mexico, surrounded by visionary petroglyphs at the Three Rivers petroglyph site, we are actually above an ancient seabed—this too is an island in what is now an ocean of air above the desert floor. To stand amid the rows of stones at Carnac is also to be in the presence of the archaic, an island demarcated by the presence of so many stones, rolling across the landscape near the sea. The archaic is itself an island. In its presence, we become more ourselves.

The great gift of John Pordage is to provide a vast metaphysics of mysticism. Of course he is part of a much larger current. His immediate predecessor is Jacob Böhme, the confluence of all the esoteric currents of the Western European tradition, alchemy, mysticism, and hermeticism. And before Böhme, there is the tradition of the great German mystics, for instance Eckhart and Tauler, and before them, Dionysius the Areopagite, before whom is the entire Platonic tradition. Pordage provides a lucid metaphysics that helps us to understand how the visible, material world is only an island within a larger context, what he terms "eternal nature," one among multiple worlds, beyond which is the vast invisible sea of the abyssal nothing.

His metaphysics suggests that our world, indeed, our cosmos, in this metaphysical context is an island. This is why so many islands are recognized as sacred, around the world, home to sacred sites, yes. But beyond that, the very nature of the island is itself highly charged, symbolic, mysterious. In some sense, all sacred sites are islands, high points in the aery currents. One sets foot on an island as a sojourner, an initiate who arrives, stays, is changed, and leaves.

Perhaps the paradigm for the initiatory nature of the island is Samothraki, home to an ancient Mystery center from before the Greeks, through Greek classical civilization and into the Roman era. There, the Mystery temple complex stood above the sea, and for millennia, initiates came and experienced the sun at midnight, and the mysteries of the polar north. For a time, initiates received an iron ring charged with the magnetic power of the place. Today, almost two millennia later, one can still feel the charge in the stones of the ruins on the island knoll above the Aegean.

A secret to the secret islands is in the stones. And here I will allude to a mystery that is visible on each one of these mysterious islands. In the traditions of the ancient kingdom of Zhang Zhung, in the Himalayas, it was held that one's life force could be guarded in a turquoise stone during life, or guided into a "soul stone" after one's physical death, after which through ritual it could be conveyed to a paradisiacal afterlife. This idea of standing stones being a vehicle for a soul's conveyance is visible also in many of the archaic traditions we have seen throughout our journeys throughout indigenous Europe, and also as far afield as Hawaii.

When we reflect again on all those mythical islands of the ancient world, including Atlantis, Hyperborea, Elysium or the Isles of the Blessed, or again Malta, Gozo, Ireland, Britain, and countless other smaller islands of the ancient European world, we are often reminded that islands, even if they are geographically known, remain mysterious, half in and half out of this world. Hence islands are associated with initiation and with the dead or with ancestors. Maybe every island is home to such secrets as can only be divulged to a few, while for the rest of us there remain just hints and legends.

We moderns tend to believe that the world is mapped, that there are no secret islands any more. And perhaps that is true, or at least, somewhat true. But I am not so cocksure of that, for I have been to enough sacred islands to know that what we see does not encompass all that actually is. There remain many mysteries in these hidden landscapes. More than once I have spoken to someone who lived for ten or twenty years near a sacred site, yet did not know where it was, or even that it existed only a short walk away. There are some islands that are more in this world than beyond it, so might there not also be islands more beyond this world than in it? Truth be told, we all live on an island of the visible in a sea of the invisible.